Praise for
Setbacks into Comebacks

Most of us will never be the army general staring down an enemy line after suffering large casualties or an NFL coach plotting their way to a Super Bowl after a difficult season, but almost all of us will suffer real-life setbacks—cancer, ailing loved ones, lost jobs, or financial hardship. Andy Billman's life script is a tutorial on how ordinary people can face extraordinary challenges with the resources we all have: the ability to say yes to opportunities, the capability to coach and be coached by our friends, family, and co-workers, and the strength to keep going when life throws us roadblocks. Andy's story is inspiring and energizing. It will make you laugh and cry and will surely help you turn your next setback into a comeback.

—Sean Murray
President of Eurofins

Taking a page from Ryan Holiday's *The Obstacle Is the Way*, Andy Billman's story is a timeless primer on how to rally and achieve success. Unfailingly personal and brutally honest, Billman opens up about the trials he faced as president of a billion-dollar business, as well as the perils of having to digest the haunting outlook of brain cancer. When life doesn't go as planned, Billman has figured out the secret of turning *Setbacks into Comebacks*.

—Brady Schlesener
Vice President of Sales and Marketing at
Gemini Group, Inc.

SETBACKS INTO COMEBACKS

Saying YES!
to Overcoming Challenges
and Embracing Opportunities

ANDY BILLMAN

ethos
collective

Printed in the United States of America

Published by Ethos Collective™
PO Box 43, Powell, OH 43065
www.ethoscollective.vip

LCCN: 2021910007
Paperback ISBN: 978-1-63680-041-7
Hardcover ISBN: 978-1-63680-042-4
E-book ISBN: 978-1-63680-043-1

Available in paperback, hardcover, e-book, and audiobook

All Scripture quotations, unless otherwise indicated, are taken from the Holy Bible, New International Version®, NIV®. Copyright © 1973, 1978, 1984 by Biblica, Inc. ™ Used by permission of Zondervan. All rights reserved worldwide.

Scripture quotations marked (NLT) are taken from the Holy Bible, New Living Translation, copyright 1996, 2004, 2015 by Tyndale House Foundation. Used by permission of Tyndale House Publishers, Carol Stream, Illinois 60188. All rights reserved.

Any Internet addresses (websites, blogs, etc.) and telephone numbers printed in this book are offered as a resource. They are not intended in any way to be or imply an endorsement by Ethos Collective™, nor does Ethos Collective™ vouch for the content of these sites and numbers for the life of this book.

Some names and identifying details have been changed to protect the privacy of individuals.

ethos
collective

DEDICATION

For Jodi, my faithful wife of thirty years, and
our four children, Ellen (Ellie), Ryan, Emily,
and Owen, along with our two grandchildren,
Will and Drew, and future grandchildren:
My love for you all is immeasurable.

CONTENTS

OFF-SEASON: HEALTH BATTLE INTO FAITH, WISDOM, AND TEACHING

FOREWORD

*Life is a journey full of challenges and obstacles,
highs and lows, ups and downs filled along
the way with many challenges, obstacles, and
opportunities. Life requires the ability to fight
and persevere—the skill to adapt and adjust.*
—Kevin Wilson

I first met Andy Billman in January 1990. Randy Walker had become the head football coach at Miami University in Ohio and brought me on as offensive line coach, specifically to work with centers and guards. We were taking over a once-proud program that had won only two games the previous two seasons. We jumped right in and went to work—hard work—trying to change the culture of the Miami football program. It was tough, it was demanding, and it was every day. Many of the returning players resisted. We lifted and ran, and we lifted and ran some more, and some more, and some more. It was not easy, and several players left the program. Those who stayed not only changed our program and built a winning foundation for Miami Football, but they also gained the skills to have successful lives and great futures.

As a twenty-eight-year-old offensive line coach at Miami, my first starting center and our team captain was Andy Billman. He worked hard and competed every day and always had a strong, positive attitude. Not only was he our starter at center, but he was also a natural team leader. He was one of the key players who helped change the attitude and direction for our team. His efforts and leadership led to a stronger culture. Our program experienced many years of success, but it all started in the spring of 1990 with Andy Billman leading the way by embracing the challenges and obstacles we faced. He and his teammates adapted, adjusted, fought hard, and persevered through many changes to establish a new era of Miami Football.

Fast forward twenty-seven years, and I am now coaching at Ohio State. My youngest son plays high school football, and after one of his summer workouts, he told me that his teammate's dad had played for me at Miami of Ohio, and his name is Billman. I thought, *You're kidding me! Andy Billman has a kid playing ball with my son. Now that's pretty cool!* A few weeks later, I was at one of my son's home games, and I saw Andy and his family in the stands (including his father, Neal, who was a Hall of Fame high school coach in Ohio). It was great to catch up. Andy looked great, and you could tell he was doing well with his personal and professional life. I felt so proud of him, although it did make me feel old!

A few weeks later, I saw Andy again at one of our son's football games, and he updated me that he had suffered a seizure while traveling on a business trip. His doctors tested and confirmed that he had brain cancer. That floored me, and I didn't know what to say. One of my players was now in for the fight of his life. I immediately began praying for Andy and his full recovery.

What I have witnessed from him these last months is what I saw from my team captain in 1990. A hard-nosed, tough guy who knows how to fight and persevere, he is now embracing the greatest of obstacles and challenges. Always able to adapt and adjust, Andy is a true winner who will fight to the end and succeed because, like all team captains, he cares more for others than he does for himself.

He was my first team captain, and he continues to live life the way he played football.

Always an inspiration.

With love and respect,
Kevin Wilson
Offensive Coordinator, Ohio State Buckeyes Football
#FIGHT #AndyBillman#52 #ProudCoach
#GoBUCKEYES

The Bene Gesserit Litany Against Fear
I must not fear.
Fear is the mind-killer.
Fear is the little-death that brings total obliteration.
I will face my fear.
I will permit it to pass over me and through me.
And when it has gone past, I will turn
the inner eye to see its path.
Where the fear has gone, there will be nothing.
Only I will remain.

NOTE TO THE READER

I've structured *Setbacks into Comebacks* into seasons—the seasons we know in football and the seasons we know in life (Preseason, Regular Season, Postseason, and Off-Season). At the end of the book, in the Appendix section, I have compiled my *Medical Notes*. By the end, I think you will be able to answer the questions, "Who is Andy Billman?" and "What is he up against?" in technical terms.

I've organized each chapter into three parts:

1. *Flash Forward* (a glimpse ahead as my journey through brain cancer ensues)

2. *Basic Narrative* (a general timeline of my life)

3. *Pause for Reflection* (an invitation to think through your own past, present, and future and identify action steps to move you forward on the timeline of your life)

I would like you to read this book as though we are sitting here chatting. We have just met and naturally are having this back-and-forth conversational volley. I tell you a piece of my story, whether it is about the time a little old lady with blue hair passed me in a marathon (Yes, that really happened.) or what happens when I don't take seizure medication. We dive into the reality of the notes from my medical team, and we reflect on our life lessons together while you share a bit of your story. I welcome you to take out your journal or write directly in this book. I invite you to read, pause, highlight, and take action.

With regard to the *Medical Notes*, I debated on whether to skim these down or keep them as is. Realizing I will have readers with a variety of experiences, I decided not to edit too much from the original text. Whether you are a patient yourself and want to compare notes or you're someone from the medical profession interested in brain cancer, you might find these helpful. They also provide a timeline of the onset of my disease through treatment.

To protect the privacy of some organizations and individuals, I have changed their names or identified them in general terms.

Without further ado, let's get started.

Hi, I'm Andy. I have brain cancer. It's been a blessing. Here's why.

PREFACE: EMERGENCY ON THE FIELD

Not all storms come to disrupt your life;
some come to clear your path.
—Unknown

MY FIRST SEIZURE

*Struggles are just a part of life. God didn't guarantee
anyone an easy life here on earth—quite the opposite.
So what are you going to do with your setbacks?
I'll tell you what you do. You make a comeback.*
—Andy Billman

Flash Forward. What's going on? Why am I seeing flashing
red and purple lights around her head? What is this woman
trying to tell me? I can see her smile, but I can't open my
mouth to engage in this friendly small talk. Why can't I
carry on this conversation? Am I making a bad impression?
I don't mean to be. I don't know what's going on with me.
Is it hot in here? My gosh, I'm sweating like crazy. I don't
feel well. My legs feel a bit wobbly. I don't want to make a
scene, but I need to get out of here. If I don't sit down—and
fast—I think I might collapse. What is happening to me?

Have you ever experienced one of those feelings when some sort of sickness is coming on? You might vomit, pass out, or both. Or maybe you have a feeling so strange that when it hits, you know only one thing—you need to get out of the place you are in. We were in Memphis, Tennessee, and had just purchased Olympic Industries, a short-run value-added metal manufacturing company. The family investment company that I represent, along with my partners, had been working on buying the company for more than a year. On our way to the company, we stopped by one of our suppliers, a coating and painting company.

After a quick tour of the facility, the owner introduced our team to his friendly wife, who also worked at the company. As I was greeting her, my vision suddenly shifted, and I saw flashing colors around her head. I felt really, really strange. I wondered if I was about to faint. I didn't know what was happening, but I knew it wasn't good. I recall it being very humid and hot.

David, one of my business partners, and our sales leader, Jeff, who had picked us up at the airport, were passing the time and chatting about famous barbecue restaurants in Memphis and country music along with all the rich history Memphis has to offer. All I could think about was how to get out of this plant without embarrassing or bringing attention to myself. I had to get to the car.

Once in the car, I became unresponsive; I could not think clearly or speak as I normally would. All I can remember about that moment was rummaging through my backpack to find a nutrition bar. Although I had never had any issues like low blood sugar, I thought that might be what was going on. I had left Columbus, Ohio, on a very early flight and had only had coffee. I figured I was simply dehydrated.

Perplexed, David and Jeff kept trying to talk to me, asking me questions to figure out what was wrong. I could not answer them, say their names, or articulate anything. I just kept saying, "Give me a minute. I just need a minute."

They later told me they were actually getting pretty upset with me. It's infuriating to try to talk to someone who won't respond. The problem, however, wasn't because I was reading my email or scrolling through Facebook on my cell phone. The problem was my brain would not work. It was the strangest feeling I had ever had. I couldn't help them. I just knew I felt weird and very off.

We have all had days where we felt off from a lack of sleep or feeling sick. This feeling was different. I literally could not think straight. I felt very confused as I tried to use my brain to figure out what was going on, not realizing my brain was the obstacle! Think of a time when you were so tired you couldn't function, or someone or something suddenly awoke you from sleep. You can see and hear what's going on around you, and you know your family, for example, but you can't engage and coherently get words out of your brain and into your mouth. Weirdly enough, I knew I was supposed to be there with David and Jeff but could not express it.

While the car's gears shifted, my brain's gears tried to figure out how to fake my way through our next stop, Olympic Industries. By that point, I couldn't even bring to mind the name of the company. I just knew we were heading to a company we owned. Like trying to grab an imaginary object floating above, my mind was racing but making no connections. Imagine yourself in a car with a group of people, riding along at an average speed. Everyone but you can read the signs along the road. You're trying desperately, but you're not even sure you can name the letters. No matter how hard you try, you can't tell anyone what the signs say.

They had enough presence of mind—thank God—to realize something was wrong; they just did not know what. They thought maybe I needed something to eat or drink, so we pulled into Chick-fil-A. *Who doesn't love Chick-fil-A in the morning?* Walking in, I was out of it, clueless as to why we were there. Jeff had me sit down while David worked to figure out what I might want to eat or drink. They kept trying to get through to me. I would not—could *not*—answer them. At that moment, I felt like I was frozen in a bad dream. I could hear them but couldn't respond. After several failed attempts to get me to communicate what I wanted to eat, David and Jeff finally decided we needed to leave and head back to the car. If I couldn't talk, I certainly wouldn't be able to eat. Fortunately for all of us, I was able to follow directions.

Back in the car, David and Jeff knew things were serious. They pulled into the first urgent care facility they saw. The catalyst for the decision had been when they asked me my wife's name. They even tried my kids' names. I knew I was married and had four children, but I couldn't provide a single name. I tried to reassure them, and just as much as I was reassuring them, I needed reassurance for myself. I can't begin to explain how strange it was to be unable to say their names. I guess I just kept saying, "It'll be okay. I'll figure it out."

At the urgent care center, I was able to walk myself in. I might as well have stayed in the car because once in and sitting, thanks to direction from David and Jeff, the woman who greeted us said, "You've got to get him to a hospital. We can't help him here." At our next stop, St. Frances Hospital, which was not far from the urgent care facility, David went up to the counter and tried to explain what was going on. By this time, the connections were gradually returning. In between the walk into the hospital and sitting down while David sought help, I began recalling each of my kids' names and a few more details. Thinking I could be suffering from a stroke, they immediately admitted me into the emergency room, during which time David and Jeff called my wife, Jodi.

The nurse brought me into a room and took me through a bunch of flashcards with pictures of different things on them. I couldn't name a card showing a picture of a cactus, which clearly represented Arizona. I knew enough to realize it was a warm place, somewhere in the "south," but couldn't come up with a word to save my life. Although I was feeling more and more like myself, I just kept repeating, "Give me a minute. Give me a minute."

After the initial failed flash card test, they scheduled me for a CT scan. Everything seemed to be happening very quickly. The only real information I received was from a nurse who told me they believed I had suffered a TIA (transient ischemic attack) stroke, also called a ministroke. Though I was familiar with the general definition of a stroke, I had no clue what a TIA stroke was. I recall asking one of the medical professionals to explain what it meant.

My initial, and perhaps slightly insensitive, thought was, *I know I'm not in the best shape, but I'm not old enough to have a stroke. Only older people have strokes; I'm only fifty!* I said this while ignoring that my kids would definitely consider fifty old! In the back of my mind—pardon the pun—I was holding onto the possibility that maybe this was all the result of getting up so early for a flight and not drinking enough water. My mother's wisdom also carried me, and I could hear her saying,

"You're fine, Andrew." Ninety-nine percent of the time, she was right, and I wasn't being tough enough, but this was clearly different.

As the symptoms dissipated, names continued coming back to me, from my business partners' first and last names to our purpose for being in Memphis, Tennessee. It was about this time that I started to come out of the fog, whatever it was. To be honest, my initial thought was it was a bunch of nothing. I couldn't help asking myself over and over, "What is going on?" Nevertheless, after the CT scan, they admitted me into the hospital and scheduled an MRI for my next test. Throughout all this, David and Jeff updated Jodi and our other partner, Nick, who was back in Columbus, and the management team at Olympic Industries. By this time, it was obvious we were not going to make our visit.

After they wheeled me back to my room, my speech had fully returned, and I had a dull headache. I was able to call Jodi at work and talk to her, but I was still very confused about what had actually happened and exactly what was going on. After talking to my doctor, I had the feeling that he wasn't sure either. Jodi, of course, said she was booking a flight to Memphis. I told her not to and that I'd be fine. I didn't want her to waste her time coming clear down to Memphis. To get to Memphis from just about anywhere requires two flights.

She knew something was wrong, though, and would not be convinced otherwise. Mothers and wives always seem to know when something is wrong. She made it to the hospital late that evening and slept in my hospital room on one of those fold-out chairs. While lying there next to her, I kept thinking, *Dear Lord, can't somebody find a way to make a more comfortable chair or bed for folks staying with loved ones at a hospital?*

The next day in the hospital brought more tests, including another MRI and an EKG. I had no idea why they kept doing all these tests. Why was I having a second MRI within twenty-four hours? The EKG was in the basement, and I remember my mind drifting and having the feeling that I was in a horror movie, deep in an old, dark basement. I thought at first I might have been hallucinating, but it was just a normal EKG test. Afterward, I returned to my room, where there were long gaps between seeing the primary doctor, waiting for test results to come back, multiple blood draws, temperature readings, IV checks, and much more. My number one thought was, *Will somebody please tell me what the #*! is going on?* You begin to feel like you are on an island waiting for a lifesaving message in a bottle. Different nurses come and go, bringing you Jell-O and other food—some edible, some not—and all you want is information!

As we sat in the hospital room, I wondered if a business idea was embedded in this lesson. Those of us in business typically cannot resist looking at everything from a business perspective. How can we improve a service or design a product to solve this problem? How can we make things better for the customer? (I am convinced that someone out there can come up with a more comfortable gown to wear in a hospital—a gown specifically for those patients who happen to be six-foot-four and 250 pounds. Something that wouldn't show his entire backside, socks that fit, maybe even decent snacks. Ice cream, anyone?)

Ever since I was in elementary school and had to visit my high-school-aged sister when she had her appendix removed, I have absolutely hated hospitals. When I saw my sister with an IV and looking very pale, I fainted. To be clear, I believe that, overall, the people who work in hospitals are wonderful, helpful, smart, and caring people. I can only imagine how hard it is to build something as large as a hospital to house scores of very sick people and meet all their individual needs at scale. I consider myself a pretty patient individual, but in that Memphis hospital, I was getting edgy, as was Jodi. We wanted answers.

On the second evening of being in the hospital, the doctor we originally talked to had consulted with his colleague, a neuro-oncologist. I never met that oncologist, but he was pretty confident I had a "glio" brain tumor after reviewing my MRIs. *Are you serious? A brain tumor?*

Most people who know me know I tend to be pretty laid back. After hearing the word tumor, raw emotions flooded my mind. Am I going to die? I don't want to leave my family. I'm not done yet. I have so much I want to do. Will I meet my new grandson? Will he even remember me after I'm gone? It was just one massive emotional moment for me. And those who know me also know that I am an emotional guy on a regular day, especially as I have gotten older. My family jokes with me about how I can't get through a wedding without crying. I will cry at a stranger's wedding! But these emotions felt intense, even for me.

After pushing aside each fear, I heard the doctor say they had deduced that I had experienced a "focal" seizure the day before. The doctor suggested we go home and get a referral to a neuro-oncologist as soon as possible. We certainly didn't object to going home! We practically had one foot out the door when we ran into roadblocks. Have you ever tried to get out of a hospital once you're admitted? It's like breaking out of Fort Knox, with mountains of forms and more waiting. The entire process had me desperate for a good old-fashioned escape!

God bless Jodi. She worked and cajoled and pushed until they finally let us leave. One of the many things I love about Jodi is that when she puts her mind to something, it is best to get out of her way. When it comes to our family, she will not take no for an answer.

Finally in the free air, we walked to our hotel about a mile away. My colleagues had returned home, and Jodi had taken a cab from the airport to come to the hospital, so we didn't have a car. There we were, running across a four-lane highway, trying to find the hotel we had reserved. For the first time in those couple of days, I laughed like a little kid. Laughter can be a great way to change your perspective, no matter your current situation.

Once settled into our hotel, we found a small place to get a late dinner. I remember breaking into more laughter and shedding more tears at that restaurant. No grown man wants to admit crying in front of anybody, but I could not hold it back (and will not hold back here with you either). All I could think about was not being with my wife of over twenty-seven years, my kids, and my family, not to mention all the wonderful friends we had both had the blessing to have over the years.

After a fitful night's sleep, we flew back to Columbus. While in flight, Jodi worked her special magic to get me into a hospital in Columbus where we might find answers and better understand what we were up against. Getting a referral to a neuro-oncologist is not exactly like ordering a pizza for delivery. These specialists' schedules are booked months in advance. Through Jodi's employment at an outpost of Nationwide Children's Hospital, she had a connection with a nurse she knew to get in touch with a doctor there. By the time our plane landed, Jodi had made it happen. We went from breaking out of the Memphis hospital to breaking into The James Cancer Hospital at Ohio State University the very next day!

We had our consultation on August 9, 2018, and by August 21, after another more extensive MRI, we had confirmation: a brain tumor. Questions still lingered on type and staging. Possibly a low-grade glioma. Doctors told us it was possible that the tumor or mass had been in my brain for years and finally had grown large enough to put enough pressure on my brain to cause a focal seizure. My doctors did not appear overly concerned. I suppose to be a good doctor, in addition to all the training and years of education, you also need a calm, cool, and collected disposition. Nobody wants to see a brain surgeon lose their cool. What was clear was that I needed surgery. They set the date in October. The news that I did not need to have my head opened up the next day was a huge relief. It also provided a much-needed sense of calmness; I reasoned that I would be in surgery sooner if they were really concerned.

I walked away from that consultation with the great doctors at OSU with a sense of confirmation, confidence, and peace. My mom's voice stayed with me: "It will be okay, you'll be okay, get back to what you were doing— your chores, your job, your life." Wisdom from my mom, who had passed away from lung cancer in 2014, along with my dad's support, love, and teaching from an early age, kicked into high gear. The support from Jodi and my entire family gave me the strength I needed to put one foot in front of the other. Resilience shifted into overdrive as I thought to myself: *We will take this as it comes, head-on. No reason to panic. No reason to stop working. The show must go on. People are counting on me.*

I think of that moment in Memphis as my wake-up call seizure because it's what tipped us off to the tumor and let us know that everything was about to change.

Pause for Reflection: Preparation

It is impossible to see around the corners and know the future, but you can prepare yourself for the inevitable setbacks in life. You can build endurance, strength, and tolerance, just as I trained myself for the marathon of brain cancer. Without knowing it, playing college football prepared me to push through the brain cancer diagnosis. With the physical grind and the mental and emotional fatigue, college football was one of the hardest trials I had ever endured.

I cannot tell you how many times I wanted to quit and just give up so I could be a normal college student. Thank God for training by my parents early on in life. In our family, it was not acceptable to give up just because something was hard. My mom's favorite thing to say to all three of us was, "You're fine, keep going."

What trials in your past have shaped you and prepared you? What stories or comments from parents, guardians, professors, or role models serve as a reminder when you need it most?

A seizure can be a warning, but it also can be debilitating. If nothing changes, what could be that seizure in your life?

PRESEASON
CHILDHOOD INTO HIGH SCHOOL

People grow through experience if they meet life honestly and courageously. This is how character is built.
—Eleanor Roosevelt

CHAPTER 1
A BIG KID NICKNAMED "BEAR"

*A good coach will make his players see what
they can be rather than what they are.*
—Ara Parseghian

Flash Forward: I'd say today is pretty rough. I just found out I have brain cancer—incurable brain cancer. As I say it in my head over and over, I can hardly believe it. Is this really happening? I've had bad days before, but this? This is terrifying. I keep taking deep breaths to calm my racing heart rate as I adjust to this news. As I gaze at my wife and the reality of it sets in, tears fall—one after the other—from my eyes as I wonder, **Am I ready for this fight**? Ready or not, I've got to fight it with all I've got. If anyone can do it, I know I can. I know who I am. My parents raised me to be courageous, confident, resilient, perseverant, and hopeful. I could be mad and resentful, but that's just not me. I'm going to fight this with the good fight of faith, knowing that God and my family are with me every step of the way. This life is fleeting, temporary, and so unexpected; therefore, it's precious. I can't sulk in this diagnosis. I won't ask **why me**. Instead, I will live each day I have to the fullest and fight this thing for my family and me. Bring on the battle.

I have realized I do not have any regrets or reservations about where I have been and who I have become. Going a step further, I believe my family is the key part of my happiness. Family then, family now. Having family around me who loves me like no one else can love me through all the dumb stuff I have done along the way. As with building a house, with the foundation in place, conviction is born. For me, that foundation is family.

And with that foundation, a "Bear" (That's me!) was born.

I was born June 28, 1968, in Westerville, Ohio, where my parents, Neal and Kay Billman, were both born and raised. They nicknamed me Bear because I was always a big kid. Despite becoming a full-scholarship, Division 1 college football player, a few words to describe my early years include clumsy, awkward, and even self-conscious. The little voice inside my head often chided me as fat. Friends and colleagues today might be surprised to learn that, to this day, I've never felt completely comfortable in my own skin. That's not easy to confess here and not something I've said aloud, aside from some big-guy jokes. But it is the truth. Body insecurity is something so many people face in one way or another, and I'm no exception.

It would be impossible to overstate the impact my mom and dad have had on me. They both worked, always industrious, whether it was my mom as a dental practice patient coordinator or volunteering for the local ambulance service where we grew up or my dad running his own painting company and chasing real estate opportunities, all while teaching and coaching at the high school level.

An only child, Mom lost her dad at an early age; he was in his fifties. She had a humble upbringing and grew up with the experience of not having a lot but always having enough. Her mom was quite successful as a manager for a reputable telephone company. Back in those days, a female leader at a decent-size company wasn't as common. My mom's strong work ethic came from watching her mother and, of course, balancing work, home, and raising three kids.

When I was a little guy, Mom volunteered with the ambulance crew. They used to laugh about my clumsiness as a youngster. Did I ever grow out of that? That's to be determined. They'd joke that it was helpful Mom was on the squad and could come by the house for my recurring episodes of getting stitches. As we got older and more independent, she continued to work. She spent many years supporting a large dental practice in Columbus, where she ensured patients had a high-quality experience from beginning to end.

My mom was a special woman, always put together with hair and makeup, organized, and tidy. She was a wonderful, petite, and smart woman. Even when fighting her cancer, she showered, dressed nicely, and put on her makeup every day. To cover the effects of chemotherapy, she added a beautiful scarf. I know she must have felt horrible, but she showed up in her best, always. Mom passed away in late 2014 after a yearlong battle with what started as lung cancer. We all miss her every day. She was so special to our family and friends and had that distinctive twinkle in her eyes when she would smile. On December 15, 2020, Jodi and I attended our granddaughter's first birthday, only four days after what would be my mom's birthday. Baby Drew Noelle has bright blue eyes just like my mom's, and I believe they are a special gift from God and my mom.

Dad is still with us today, in great health, and living in southwest Florida from October to early May and in northern Michigan from mid-May through late September. He's the youngest of three boys. When Dad was young, his parents divorced, and fortunately, they had a grandfather who did more than just keep an eye on them. From my dad's stories, I know that he and his brothers grew up with little money. They had a good deal of freedom and found their share of trouble. Dad was a three-sport athlete, although football and basketball were his best. When talking about his teen years, he often laughs and says that he would probably be in jail if it were not for sports. He's mostly joking, of course, but growing up in the 1950s without much adult supervision certainly offered a lot of opportunity for mischief.

After surviving high school, Dad joined the marines at Parris Island, South Carolina. He doesn't talk much about his time in the US Marine Corps, but being a marine was a catalyst and turning point for attaining more discipline and direction in his life. After his service, Dad earned his master's degree at Ohio State and became a high school teacher and football coach at Upper Arlington in Ohio. There he was part of a very special group of high school coaches and players in Columbus who won multiple state titles in the 1960s. Later he became the head coach in Gahanna, Ohio. Dad's career led him to an induction into the Ohio Coaches Hall of Fame. Following his career in education and coaching, he served as a vice president of State Savings Bank in Columbus for twenty-plus years before retiring when a larger, publicly held regional bank took over. Though it might seem strange that a high school football coach and teacher could transition into banking, Dad flourished in that job. He had a special gift to lead teams and motivate people to reach their God-given ability, so it is no surprise that he was so successful in the business world.

Before Mom passed away, they had celebrated fifty-plus years of marriage. Their marriage wasn't perfect. What marriage is? Marriage takes work, with each spouse growing along the way. Someone once said that there are times when one spouse needs to carry the burden for the whole marriage. Which I suppose is why the vows include "for better or worse."

I'm sure it was not easy to raise three kids amidst all the games and transitions, but we felt their genuine love for each other and for us. All three of us are now married with children. My older brother, Mike, and his wife, Kathy, have two adult kids and live near us in Columbus. My sister, Beth, and her husband, Dave, have four kids and live in Cincinnati. I'm the youngest, and my wife, Jodi, and I have four kids.

Much of my daily motivation comes from my parents. My siblings and I grew up in a safe but humble environment. We had a good deal of freedom because they were always working to support our family and pursue their own passions in life. While the cat's away, the mice will play! I remember exploring, swimming, camping, and spending many a day with my friends, often in the woods, miles away, but *not* before getting my chores done. My sister and brother love to say they had it a lot harder growing up than I did. They were right. The baby of the family often ends up having it a little easier. After having had a couple of kids, I think it's just natural to let the third or fourth child get away with more. I was no exception—no mandatory piano lessons or Boy Scouts for me!

I'm grateful for growing up in the 1970s and '80s. It was just a cool time to be alive. Leaving the house for the whole day or sleeping out in the woods was completely normal back then. I would tell my mom or dad where I was going and who all was going along, but there were no iPhones or Androids with built-in GPS locators back then. My parents simply trusted that I would be back for dinner. We also lived in a great, safe neighborhood with tons of young boys around. We were always playing backyard football or shooting hoops in someone's driveway.

We made our own fun, experiencing life in a hands-on way, exploring the world around us, and just being kids without our parents hovering over us and dictating every step. I'm not finding fault with today's parents. Times have simply changed.

When Jodi and I began having kids, we felt the shift in the parenting safety net. We had Ellen, our first, in 1993, and although it was a long time ago, things had changed quite a lot from when we grew up. I cannot recall a time when we didn't know exactly where Ellen or any of our kids were; they were either with us, at a trusted friend's house, or at school. There just was not a time when any of my kids wandered around the neighborhood on their own or out exploring in the woods. If that happened today, I think Jodi and I might have gone to jail!

When it comes to the guidance, boundaries, and freedom we give our kids, the key word is *balance*. Although things have changed in our world, and technology is now at the forefront, I personally think letting kids explore and figure things out on their own can be a positive thing. It goes without saying that it wasn't that my parents didn't love us or worry about us; they simply provided the freedom to learn and grow on our own.

With what I'd call a nice, normal childhood, Mom and Dad instilled discipline and taught us the value of hard work from an early age. Mom worked five days a week, and it seemed like Dad was always working, especially when he was building his coaching career. When he became a head coach in 1970, it was completely normal for him to be gone to school from early in the morning to late in the evening. After practice, he would swing home for a quick family meal and then spend many more hours watching film of the Gahanna Lincoln Lions and preparing for their upcoming opponents.

Although he loved coaching and was incredibly passionate about positively impacting young men's lives, after considering a move into the college coaching ranks, Dad ended up embracing an opportunity to jump into the business world. Back in the mid-1970s, high school teachers and coaches did not make a lot of money. In my opinion, they are still underpaid. For my dad, having three kids who aspired to go to college someday created an additional incentive to pursue financial opportunity. He was always learning, growing, and moving forward, which made him open to the career pivot.

With Dad's work at the bank, my parents had a little more in their pockets to show their eclectic taste. They bought a unique 1800s home with tons of character. Nestled on three acres, it was out in the country but still very close to school. It was a cool place for me to spend my last couple of elementary school years and all the way through high school. After I was out of college and married with kids, my parents purchased an eight-acre island named Quarry Island on the Potagannissing Bay in Northern Michigan, almost to Canada. My dad lives there in the summer months and is always hard at work making it better. His mindset is to pay it forward for the next generation, especially now that he has ten grandchildren and two great-grandchildren.

As a gritty, hard-working family guy, I admire my dad. At eighty-two, he still gets plenty of exercise, walking and playing tennis against different opponents, some almost half his age—he's still in it to win it. He might be in his eighties, but in health, he looks like a vibrant fifty-year-old! As strong and active as he is, it still has been hard to see him age and especially to watch my mom fight for her life and ultimately leave us. She was so resilient, never complained, and was such a role model for what I am going through now. I attribute much of my endurance to her. So much of my drive, business interest, and focus on family comes from my mom and dad. I am grateful every day for the life they have given me and for the work ethic that came from their expectations.

Pause for Reflection: Action

Positive or negative, where we come from leads to where we go and who we are. My parents always instilled in us the attitude of striving to be your best in whatever you do, of pursuing happiness and excellence in life. As revealed in the Will Smith movie, *The Pursuit of Happyness*, if we are honest with ourselves, many of us think life owes us something or that happiness is guaranteed.

How have your experiences shaped your life? Where are you now?

What actions can you take to move forward and find happiness, despite your circumstances?

If, for some reason, you missed an aspect of your childhood, choose to flip your paradigm. You can embrace life now, have fun, learn, grow, be curious, and find yourself in ways you never thought you could!

Embrace life now, have fun, learn, grow, and be curious.

CHAPTER 2
I'M GLAD I DID MY CHORES

Count that day lost whose descending sun
finds you with no good deeds done.
—Napoleon Hill (and frequently
repeated by Neal Billman)

The Need for Self-Discipline: *Do you not know that in*
a race, all the runners run, but only one gets the prize?
Run in such a way as to get the prize. Everyone who
competes in the games goes into strict training. They
do it to get a crown that will not last, but we do it to
get a crown that will last forever. Therefore I do not
run like someone running aimlessly; I do not fight like
a boxer beating the air. No, I strike a blow to my body
and make it my slave so that after I have preached to
others, I myself will not be disqualified for the prize.
—1 Corinthians 9:24–27

Flash Forward: Well, that's going to be a shiner, all right. Ow! My seizure medication wreaked havoc on me, yet again. Chuckle. I'm not quite as steady and aware as I used to be, which could be the reason I tried to walk through the wall instead of the doorway on my way to the bathroom last night. These meds make me groggy and disoriented at times, causing these mishaps. What else can I do but laugh? There's nothing I can do about it now except cover the wound with a spiffy butterfly bandage and carry on with my day. I have too many blessings in my life to allow little obstacles like this to ruin our vacation with our best friends. In fact, I refuse to let any obstacle get in my way of finishing my race—and finishing it strong.

I remember being twelve, maybe thirteen, years old and learning how to do the family ironing, including hanging up the clothes. And, yes, I can still iron! Whatever needed to be done—setting the table for dinner and putting the napkins and silverware in the right place, doing loads of laundry, mowing the lawn, even some cooking—I could do it. Okay, I never did any *serious* cooking, but I did follow my mom's explicit instructions, written on a note on our countertop, to put the casserole in the oven at 450 degrees at 5:00 p.m. My specialty, mind you, was grilled cheese, and I could make a wicked bowl of cereal too.

This wasn't just a summer thing either; the Billman kids had daily responsibilities. Plenty of fun, plenty of freedom, plenty of time with buddies, but also plenty of work and chores to go around. Daily, in addition to whatever chores Dad gave us, Mom would give a to-do list as she headed out the door to work. It is amazing how much of that early childhood training is embedded into my life, even today as a fifty-two-year-old dad and businessman. It is okay to have expectations for your kids to pitch in and fulfill household needs. As Admiral William H. McRaven shared in his 2014 commencement address at the University of Texas, if you want to change the world, start with making your bed every day.

We also learned early on to be finishers, never to do things halfway. You do not rake the garden and leave the rake in the garden—you put it away. The Billman boys do the dishes, and that includes Dad pitching in. But one particular day, when Mike and I left the table too early to play, Dad firmly corrected, "You boys will finish the dishes." From that point on, we had set days for that specific chore. My brother and I still fight over whose day it is to do the dishes when we are at each other's houses. Because of my upbringing, my goal every day is to finish. Whatever race it might be, I will finish.

> My goal every day is to finish. Whatever race it might be, I will finish.

It amazes me how embedded these early childhood lessons are to this day—make your bed, dress properly for the occasion, and do your chores before goofing around. We tend to complicate parenting, but we can keep it simple with consistent expectations. Jodi and I have tried to continue a similar set of structures in our home.

Being tough on our kids can be challenging but worth it to make them responsible and productive in the home and all they pursue in life. And don't get me wrong, I can be a mighty big softy. I often talk with Jodi and others about how I have been too soft on my kids, partly because of my personality and partly due to growing up in a disciplined environment. In our household, thankfully, Jodi has been stronger at being tough on the kids, and we have found our balance in doing our best as parents.

My dedication to completing tasks, however, didn't cross over into developing greater coordination as I grew. Though I would later develop into a successful athlete and leader, I was a klutz as a kid. I was clumsy and forgetful, yet content and easygoing. My memories of family vacations recall images of me being goofy and Mom shaking her head at my forgetfulness or clumsiness. There is not an elegant bone in my body, which is evident from the medical art formed by all the stitches and scars I've collected.

Once while carrying in pop bottles from the store, I managed to trip on the first step up to the house, break all the bottles, and cut my hand. I can still see Mom shaking her head and saying, "Andrew, what are you doing?" She was constantly taking me somewhere to get stitches. I should have had a punch card for a set of free stitches! On one vacation to Florida, I slipped on the pool deck and busted my chin open. And then there was the time I stood between two vehicles, put my hands on both cars, and proceeded to do a flip. You guessed it—I busted my chin open again, requiring multiple stitches. I do not recommend trying that at home.

And then there were the times when my mind just wandered, and I lost things. For example, during middle school, we went on a family vacation to Williamsburg, Virginia. Mom gave specific instructions to take our Sunday best when packing to leave, including our nice shoes because we'd be going out to dinner at a very nice restaurant. This is an example of the many lessons my parents constantly taught on etiquette. We were to behave as though we were meeting the Queen of England: dress your best, sit up straight, look people in the eye, and be polite.

When I started to pack, I realized I had lost my nice shoes. *Oh, no. I'll have to fake it.* I went into Dad's closet and grabbed a pair of his shoes, which were at least two sizes too big. But I figured I could hide my way through losing the shoes—as I did with every pair. On the evening of the special dinner, we all got dressed, and Mom and I were in the elevator when she finally got a good look at my attire. "Andrew! Whose shoes are you wearing? Are those your father's?" I can still see her shaking her head and giving me that here-we-go-again glare. She was right, of course. That old saying, "If your head weren't attached, you'd lose it," was written just for me.

And then there's my brother Mike, who is three years older and wasn't so easy on me. For example, in high school, we were physically going at it, like most brothers do, with a good round of punches. I ended up on the pavement. Mom called Dad at work and told him he needed to come home because, in her words, "I can't control them anymore."

Though he takes the credit for me later getting a college football scholarship, I lovingly offer him that credit where it is due. I was a passive kid, and he toughened me up, no doubt. And for that, I say to little Mike, "Thank you, and do note: I kept all my hair. Look at this beautiful head of hair, Mike!" (In case it wasn't clear, my brother has parted ways with most of his.)

Although football will always be my go-to sport, I played basketball in fifth and sixth grades. I loved the game! Perhaps I should have ended my career there. It was not good, not good. Once in high school, while transitioning from football season to basketball season, I accidentally took out the star center (who was slated to play varsity, by the way) by clumsily fouling and breaking his hand while he was taking a shot. I just hacked him—a total Neanderthal move. He and I still laugh about it today. As you can imagine, our coaches were *not* happy with me. My basketball career ended after that season.

In addition to basketball and football, I went out for cross-country and track. In eighth grade, I joined cross-country, thanks to a crush on a girl. What the heck was I thinking? Not only was she on the cross-country team, but she was also the fastest runner! When I realized it was not for me and I tried to quit, it was too late. Mom made me finish. And finish, I did. Last in every meet. Embarrassing. Once in high school, I tried track and competed in the shot put. I was horrible, but that's okay. I learned what it meant to try and finish—even when I absolutely disliked the sport, event, or season. I finished.

These early chores, events, and seasons would set me up for the big events I would face later on in my journey. Mom and Dad expecting the finish early on is something that became ingrained in me, a part of my DNA. Saying yes to finishing was the biggest and most important life lesson I learned, and is one I would model and teach.

Count That Day Lost

If you sit down at set of sun
And count the acts that you have done,
And, counting, find
One self-denying deed, one word
That eased the heart of him who heard,
One glance most kind
That felt like sunshine where it went—
Then you may count that day well spent.
But if, through all the livelong day,
You've cheered no heart, by yea or nay—
If, through it all
You've nothing done that you can trace
That brought the sunshine to one face—
No act most small
That helped some soul and nothing cost—
Then count that day as worse than lost.

—George Eliot, 1887

Pause for Reflection: Finishing the Race

A lot of people experience setbacks and give up on life. They get morose and take it out on other people. I believe setbacks are when God wants us to see how we are learning, growing, and catalyzing to turn the setback into a comeback.

What race are you in that you are struggling to finish?

To finish a race, we must resolve to keep going and develop an attitude of perseverance. Throughout the multiple setbacks I have had in my life, this has probably been the most inspiring and simple thing to remember.

> To finish a race, we must resolve to keep going and develop an attitude of perseverance.

When in your life have you been held to the standard of finishing? From childhood? Early adulthood? Later?

What will finally crossing that finish line mean to you?

CHAPTER 3
HIGH SCHOOL, FOOTBALL, & HIGH SCHOOL SWEETHEART

I love you not only for what you are but for what I am when I am with you. I love you not only for what you have made of yourself but for what you are making of me.
—Roy Croft

Flash Forward: As I sit here gathering my thoughts for this chapter, I'm moved to tears as I think of my wife, Jodi, who is my rock—strong and unwavering in the face of adversity. My brain cancer is one heck of a diversion in what we imagined our life to be, and I cannot imagine the fear and anxiety Jodi must have felt when she got the call about my first seizure. Yet this beautiful, compassionate woman, who is the love of my life, weathers all the storms with me. As we face challenges again and again, we continue to withstand the test of time.

When basketball did not work out, football became my focus. Being bigger than most of the guys, I played as an offensive tackle at Gahanna High School from 1982 through 1986. I worked my way up from playing junior varsity on Saturdays to varsity on Friday nights. In addition to being a co-captain my senior year, which meant a lot to me, I made All-State in Ohio and played in the all-star football game at the end of the season.

My dedication to football paid off, and I owe so much to my high school coach, Phil Koppel, who campaigned on my behalf. He sent films, made calls, and opened the school for coaches to visit and meet me. That was such a fun time for me, and I'd come home to these letters from colleges. It was a big deal to me to have these big schools considering me for a scholarship, and I never took that for granted. Northwestern University, Indiana University, University of North Carolina, Ohio State University, Vanderbilt University, and West Point were all reaching out. Northwestern offered a full scholarship, but I ultimately chose Miami of Ohio.

I was humbled and honored to have an opportunity to play for Miami. The fact that my mom started at Miami—and both my brother and sister attended—was icing on the cake. Many people asked me why I did not try to play in the Big Ten, especially after receiving the scholarship to Northwestern. My answer was simple. At that young age, I had a pretty good sense of my skills and future football career. At six-foot-four and maybe 245 pounds, I was also on the small side for an offensive lineman. Today a Division 1 lineman can easily be six-foot-six and well over 300 pounds, yet still move like a cat and bench 500-plus pounds. I did not want to be one of those guys who rode the bench for four years and only got to play when the team was up by forty points. I wanted to play! Miami was the perfect fit for me.

Sports were not the only thing that had my attention in high school. *Back to the Future* became my first-date story with my high school sweetheart, Jodi Hochuli. After that, we went on a double date with my best friend, who would later be my college roommate in our fraternity, and Jodi's best friend, still great friends of ours today. Jodi would later become the love of my life, my wife, and the driving force in our family, especially when it counted most during our trials.

Jodi and I met on the Fourth of July. We dated my senior year when she was a junior, and then I was off to college. Once Jodi graduated high school, she began working as a travel agent and a medical leasing company for dental practices. When she could, she'd jump in her diesel Volkswagen Rabbit on Fridays right after work, drive down to Miami, and we would hang out. We did this through my five years of college (more on that fifth year later).

Jodi came from a devout Catholic home, and her parents grew up with a humble background, much like my parents, and started a big family of four with a similar upbringing. They are two of the most gracious, loving, and giving people I've been blessed to know. I've heard many stories of bad in-laws, and my situation is the polar opposite. Jodi's drive and resilience resulted from her upbringing and her struggles as a learner in school. Compared to our school years, education has evolved to accommodate the diversity in students' learning styles.

Teaching and learning are not a one-size-fits-all approach. Today's educators are equipped with countless tools to successfully teach and guide students, regardless of each learning style. When learners struggle, they have to find ways to compensate, and Jodi's response to her trials included hard work and discipline. She opted out of college and headed straight to work and has always been industrious and done well at every endeavor. Today she works for Nationwide Children's Hospital in Columbus.

You might be surprised to learn I was a good student and, okay, a bit of a theater junkie. I enjoyed football, but I knew my chances of playing the game professionally were zero, so why not get involved in other things? My buddies often teased me, "Billman, *what* are you doin'?" I did enjoy taking part in our high school theater called Varsity Varieties. In fact, I invited the teasing during one particular act as a member of The Village People. The cheerleaders had taught us football players a routine, and I split my pants during the show. As you can imagine, that, of course, led to more rounds of "Billman, *what* are you doin'?"

As a kid, I was slow and weak, but as I mentioned earlier, I was always a bigger kid and continued to be a bigger guy during my high school years. My physique led me to receive the nickname "Bundy," after the WWF wrestler, King Kong Bundy. King Kong Bundy (Christopher Alan Pallies) was this massively huge guy—and wrestling legend, I might add. He later became a comedian and went into acting and was especially beloved by his wrestling colleagues and stars like the Hulk. If the shoe fits.

I have always been a pretty easygoing guy, even if serving as the brunt of the joke. I honestly think a big part of my ability to continually recover from tough situations is related to my innate ability to laugh at myself. A healthy sense of humor can carry you a long way in life. Life is mainly a struggle along the way. Life can be hard enough as it is—why not let some of those tough situations roll off your back and just keep going?

Pause for Reflection: Relationships and Humor

Who we become gets its start within our relationships, whether with family, friends, or significant others. For Jodi and me, this was the start of our relationship. With everything we have been through, I cannot imagine life without her.

Take a moment and consider who that person is in your life. Who has withstood the test of time alongside you?

I can't leave this chapter without touching on the need for humor. Do not be so hard on yourself. A good sense of humor can help you get through life.

> Do not be so hard on yourself. A good sense of humor can help you get through life.

Where do you see your sense of humor on a scale of one to ten: toward life in general, toward yourself? If you don't have that sense of humor now, how can you work to develop it?

REGULAR SEASON
COLLEGE INTO CAREER

*It's not whether you get knocked
down; it's whether you get up.*
—Vince Lombardi

CHAPTER 4

FROM BENCHED TO "SHOULD I QUIT?" TO IN THE GAME

We can rejoice, too, when we run into problems and trials, for we know that they help us develop endurance, and endurance develops strength of character, and character strengthens our confident hope of salvation.
—Romans 5:3–4 (NLT)

Flash Forward: Today, as I push through the pain, nausea, and discomfort I'm experiencing as a result of my treatment, I'm tempted to reflect on where my strength, my hope, and my optimism comes from. Because even though they say this brain cancer isn't going away, I somehow keep telling myself, *Keep going, Andy. Keep moving. You can beat this. You may be small, weak, and slow, but God is not!*

In the fabric of my resilient character, I see my parents and the life values they taught me. I see football and my coach, who saw in me things I didn't see in myself. I see the disappointments and injuries that fueled my passion and desire to never give up. I see my career that had such unexpected, difficult twists and turns and taught me things I didn't know I needed to learn. I look back and realize this is me. This is what I do. It's a part of my DNA. I turn setbacks into comebacks.

Miami University of Ohio held special meaning for my family and me. My mom attended, and Mike and Beth both met their spouses and graduated from there. Over the years, that legacy continued with more Billmans—my nieces, nephews, and two of our kids—from the next generation attending Miami of Ohio.

When I arrived at Miami as a freshman in 1986, I quickly learned how difficult it was to be a scholarship athlete, balance new relationships, and do well in college. For everyone who goes away to college and rooms with someone new, a story is bound to happen. My roommate, Dave, a tough Polish kid and a bit of a wild man, was from the south side of Chicago. When I first met him, he asked, "So you're from Ohio? How many cows does your family have?"

"Dude, my dad's a banker," I said before busting out in laughter. We ended up rooming together for three years and becoming great friends. Dave went on to become a teacher and moved to Hawaii with his wife. As freshmen, we both redshirted and were relegated to the football team's practice squad our first year. During one practice, Dave, a linebacker, and I knocked each other out during a drill where we were matched up. Affectionately nicknamed the "hamburger drill," it consisted of running as fast as you could into another person. It was a daily drill that the coaches relished as a great way to separate the weak from the strong. The bottom line was my roommate and I hit each other so hard with our helmets that we knocked each other out and both ended up with mild concussions.

Being recruited to be a guard was truly a humbling experience. I came in as this *big fish*, the all-conference scholarship athlete from a small town. I got to know myself deeply that first year and what it meant to discipline myself to work hard, and I thought about quitting several times. Aside from the academic challenge, college football was the hardest thing I'd ever faced. I'll never forget a defensive coach being particularly upset with me for not being tough enough. He absolutely embarrassed me in front of all the upperclassmen, including my fellow redshirts.

Being a redshirt literally meant you wore a red mesh shirt over your jersey to indicate you were a lowly scout team player to be pushed around by the starters. They break you down. That coach called me names I'd never even heard of before—and, trust me, aren't for this book. In one minute, Coach figured out what would push me to be tougher, play harder, and go longer.

I learned an important lesson that first day on the field about motivation and the psychology of a man: Motivation must come from within a person. *You* have to be the one to ultimately make a change or push through a circumstance. I have always been a mild-mannered, easygoing guy. Coach knew that about me and figured out how to push the right buttons to activate my inner ignition. He had a knack for it. He stimulated the want-to attitude inside me. Sometimes people just need that extra nudge to overcome the *obstacle* standing in their way.

> Motivation must come from within a person. *You* have to be the one to ultimately make a change or push through a circumstance.

That type of motivation is a gift, and I could write an entire chapter about my coach alone! As I reflect on my redshirt year, I think about how I pushed myself to learn, grow, and study. It was during this time that I prepared myself for coming off the bench.

Miami won the Mid-American Conference that year with eight wins and four losses. We beat LSU, which was ranked eighth in the country, at LSU and went on to play at the California Bowl. Being a redshirt, I didn't get to travel. Sitting in my dorm room and watching it on TV became a catalyst to take my game to the next level. I wanted to participate and be part of something special going forward. I've always wanted the ball, always wanted to be a leader, always wanted to be out front and on the field. Hanging in the background or playing in someone else's shadow has never been my preference.

During my sophomore year, I ditched my red shirt and finally found my strength zone, but not without another curveball. "Billman, you're now going to be a center," Coach said to me after another center had hurt his knee. I had only snapped a football one time before in the All-Ohio high school game. I could have resisted, told Coach, "No thanks. I'll stay where I am." But there I was—going from offensive lineman to learning how to be a center in my second year, and I loved every minute of it. I said, "YES."

Truth be known, I was always the small, slow, and weak (in terms of physical strength) guy the entire time I was at Miami. I played the game at a max of 265 pounds, which was a lot of weight to carry for a slow player who stood six-foot-four. At the same time, however, I played the game smart and made the best of my ability to call the line play, be in the right position at the right time, and not make mistakes. I did not play a lot my sophomore year, but I did get in the game. I remember playing against Miami of Florida, where future Dallas Cowboy and now Hall of Famer Michael Irvin played. At the infamous Miami vs. Miami game, we got clobbered, 54-3. Miami of Florida finished undefeated and won the national championship against Oklahoma that year. We finished with a 5-6 record, but at least we had scored a field goal against the soon-to-be national champs.

Pause for Reflection: Personal Development

We do not want to be benched, but sometimes God benches us. We do not understand it at the time. We think we are ready, but we aren't ready until we are in the fire. I have consistently struggled with setting unrealistic expectations for myself. I am learning to recognize this pattern and hit the pause button, even for a short while. We sometimes need to take the time to reflect, reassess our goals and priorities, and then regroup.

When have you felt benched?

Little trials prepare us for big trials. What is big at the time may seem small in comparison, but if we develop our endurance and strength of character, we will be prepared for the trials that will truly challenge our physical, mental, and emotional spirit. What trials have you faced?

Little trials prepare us for big trials.

CHAPTER 5

INJURY WILL NOT STOP ME: MY POSITION, MY RESPONSIBILITY

*Today I will do what others won't, so tomorrow
I can accomplish what others can't.*
—Jerry Rice, Hall of Fame Wide Receiver, 49ers

Flash Forward: I slowly open my eyelids, awaking to the birds chirping outside my window. I can see the red and orange glow of the sun rising in the east. I turn and see my beautiful, precious bride sleeping peacefully next to me. A gentle smile forms as I take a deep breath and silently pause with deep, sincere gratitude to God for the gift of yet another day. A day to kiss my wife. A day to love my kids. A day to play with my grandbabies. A day to impact others positively. A day to make a difference. A day to not just live this life I've been given, but to live it to the fullest.

It's strange even to think this, but getting brain cancer is the greatest blessing of my life. It's causing me to evaluate the true meaning of life and choose how I want to live it. Anyone can be happy or satisfied when things are going great (job, marriage, kids, whatever it may be), but it's so much harder when things are going wrong. So as I wake for yet another day of life—remembering all the struggles, hardships, and setbacks that have brought me to this moment, with this perspective—I'm committed to putting my feet firmly on the floor and turning them into comebacks. I'm committed to living my best life today.

Before the 1988–1989 season started, I needed to get a wrist treated that I had broken in the prior season. I had injured it in practice, at which time I was a backup. Our athletic trainers had fashioned a plastic piece to wear on my wrist, along with a significant amount of athletic tape to hold the piece together so that I could practice and play the entire season. As a backup, I did not get a lot of game-playing time that year, but I knew someone was right behind me who wanted the starting job the next season. The broken bone was on my left, non-snapping wrist. It required a bone graft that the doctor took from my hip, which we did after the season ended, so I could practice in the spring and fight to win the starting spot. I learned how to play injured and with pain. Football can be a brutal sport. It is not for the faint of heart.

I had my surgery back home over Christmas break. Much to my lack of fortune, I did not leave the hospital in perfect condition. I left with the chickenpox. Yes, the chickenpox! It just would not be a comeback story without Andy Billman getting the chickenpox! I will never forget calling my mom at work while I was home recuperating in a total panic, "Mom, I have got all these weird spots all over my body. I can't stop itching. What the heck is wrong with me?"

I recall a long pause on the phone and then Mom coming back with, "Andy, you have the chickenpox." She thought I had contracted it when I was much younger, but maybe it had been a mild case. *Chickenpox? What the hell?* Mom told me to take a bath and pour oatmeal in the water. I was like, *Oatmeal? Really? Seriously, why would I put Quaker Oats in the bathtub?* I thought my mom was crazy, but, of course, she was not. Mothers truly know best. The oatmeal was great for calming down a bad itch, and I swam in Quaker Oats for a week until the itching subsided.

Entering my third year at Miami, I earned the starting spot at center. Let's just put it out there now—we finished 0-10-1. We were horrible, last in the conference. Talk about being humbled. During that terrible season, while playing at Minnesota, I sprained my ankle badly. That was back in the day when a lot of football fields were artificial turf, which was notorious for causing sprained ankles and torn ligaments of all types. Natural grass, which simply has more give than fake turf, is kinder to football cleats. After that game, I limped back to the hotel and slept with a cold pack on my ankle. Although I had to sit out the fourth quarter of that game, and we got beat, all I could think about was how not to relinquish my starting position the following week.

I knew that many other guys wanted my job, and I was unwilling to give it up. My power of persistence was born. I pulled motivation from deep within to push through the pain and discomfort and hang in there. My fight alone, however, could not save my football team from a losing season.

Today I honor all of those setbacks because they helped me fight through brain cancer and find the strength to come back from brain surgery, radiation, and chemotherapy.

In my fourth year, as a senior and once again a starting center, we finished with a record of 2-8-1. Not as bad, but not where I would like us to have been, of course. The school fired our coach, Tim Rose, and I wanted to quit. My dad surprisingly left that decision up to me. I expected some pushback, but he was teaching me an important life lesson in Coach Billman form. He let me know I was old enough to make my own decision, allowing me to pick a path with conviction. That lesson has served me well my entire life. Miami hired former star offensive player Randy Walker who had been on a string of winning Miami teams. He returned to his alma mater from North Carolina, where he had been a successful assistant coach.

The irony was that Coach Walker had tried to recruit me back in high school to go to North Carolina. Once on Miami's campus, he asked me to come into his office and convinced me to come back for my fifth season of eligibility. I was all in. During the off-season, I was back home, painting houses to make extra money. Before going back to Miami for my fifth season, Jodi and I got engaged. By that time, we had been dating for more than five years. We set our wedding date for May 11, 1991.

Under Coach Walker, I experienced my toughest year of preseason workouts. We went from doing aerobics in the basketball arena the year before to running stairs in the stadium until we puked. During this season, I learned even more about myself than I had in the previous seasons combined. Prior to this off-season workout program, I would have considered myself a pretty hard-working individual. I had no clue. I suppose none of us do until we push ourselves to the limit. That season I learned we all need to continue to push to match our natural God-given capability. I gained a true sense of work ethic and what it takes to be a winner at anything in life, not just football. That season my peers elected me to be offensive team captain.

After overcoming the broken wrist surgery, getting chickenpox, and spraining an ankle, more setbacks were just around the corner. In my fifth season, I smashed my finger into someone else's helmet during a Thursday night practice. The doctor's recommendation was to get stitches—on my snapping hand. We had a game on Saturday, though, and there was *no way* I would be missing the game. They wrapped it up as best they could. Oh. Man. It hurt like hell every time I snapped the ball to my quarterback during that game, but I persevered and told myself it was worth it. *My position. My responsibility. I was not giving anyone else my job.*

For a while, though, a little voice inside considered letting someone else take over my position, even if for a little bit. It's okay to have those thoughts. Sometimes just thinking about giving up motivates you to stick to your path. Life is hard, and most jobs are competitive by nature. That is one of the many things that makes our country great. Most of us need to fight and grind each and every day to keep our jobs.

Team sports, including football, mold you like most things cannot. In my humble opinion, with the exception of our military, which teaches men and women to protect our freedoms every day, there is no better preparation for life, business, marriage—or you name it—than playing a team sport. I love the military analogy of "holding the line"—whether it be a World War II or Vietnam War story of soldiers pushing back the enemy and holding their ground. I felt that way in football and would think, *Andy, you can't let another guy take your spot. You must hold the line. No matter how much it hurts.* Throughout all the accidents, injuries, and pain of my childhood and high school and college years, my resilience served me well, and I owe that to my parents. In our family, you had to have a serious flesh wound to miss school. The phrase in our house was, "You're fine, you're fine. Keep going."

I applied that mantra while fighting to earn my business degree. Calculus was particularly difficult for me, and I dropped out and had to take it a second time, barely passing with a D. With calculus, accounting, economics, and football, I struggled mightily, but I made it through.

That season our team made a comeback and finished at 5-5-1. To most people, going 5-5-1 in any comparable sport is not exactly noteworthy. Context matters. For our team under Coach Walker, it was a year of turning around the bus. From a winless team just two years before, we demonstrated that Miami was capable of competing again for the MAC (Mid-American Conference) championship. And with that, I graduated in December 1990 with a degree in business.

Pause for Reflection: Perseverance

Although it is hard to compare breaking a bone in college football to brain cancer, the point is the same. When life does not go our way, we need to hold the line. We need to be strong, resilient, persistent, hopeful, and optimistic. I will be the first to admit that's easy to say but very hard to do.

> When life does not go our way, we need to hold the line. We need to be strong, resilient, persistent, hopeful, and optimistic.

When has life showed up and hit you hard, how did you respond?

Although I advocate pushing back at whatever is hurting you, it is also good to take a pause and take care of yourself. After you rest for a bit, get back after it, whatever you are fighting. Whether it is cancer or some other attack, it always seems to hit us when we are most vulnerable.

If a life setback has happened to you, a friend, or a family member, do you recall a time when you or others persevered and pushed through? How did you manage to get to the other side of the crisis?

Regardless of temperament, we all have an inner strength we must learn how to access when we need it.

CHAPTER 6
WAKE-UP CALL

Sow a thought and you reap an action; sow an act and you reap a habit; sow a habit and you reap a character; sow a character and you reap a destiny.
—Ralph Waldo Emerson

Flash Forward: Hand-in-hand, we walk slowly, yet assertively, through the hospital hallways lined with doctors, nurses, and patients. It feels strange to think I was here just a couple of weeks ago for brain surgery, where we heard I have brain cancer. We know it isn't good. Our somber facial expressions clearly announce the ache of our new reality. We've done our research. We have an idea of what we are up against, but we have so many questions. Is there treatment? Will the tumor grow back? What causes this? How much time do I have?

I squeeze Jodi's hand as we enter the neuro-oncology unit. I try to calm my nerves and the overwhelm of the unknown with deep breaths, prayer, and positive thinking as we sit waiting for the doctor to come in and talk to us about my options. I'm so curious to learn everything I can about this diagnosis so I can go to battle. Finally, I hear the door open, and in walks the doctor. Jodi and I greet him with an anxious, "Hello," but our minds are rushing with all kinds of thoughts. It's hard to calm my mind and focus.

We lean in and begin to soak up every word he says. "You have incurable brain cancer. Most likely, it will come back. If it does, you can have surgery again." My immediate response is, "What about now? What can we do now to prolong my life?" He proceeds to tells us the standard of care involves radiation and chemo. Before I give it much thought and before I have a chance to discuss it with Jodi, I blurt out, "Yes to all of it! Give it to me now. The radiation. The chemo. As fast as you can." Jodi looks at me. "Are you sure? Don't you want to talk about this first?" Knowing this hurts her, I give her a look with nothing but deep, incredible love and compassion in my eyes and simply respond, "Yes, I'm sure." I grab her hand, look up at the doc, and ask, "When can we start?"

After graduation, I packed Barney Rubble—my car—and headed to my parent's home in Powell, Ohio. After five years of nonstop college football and academics, I was enjoying my freedom and hanging out with Jodi and my friends while I looked for a full-time job that winter.

I had an interview lined up with Sherwin-Williams in Cleveland and was chasing a few other options when I got a wake-up call. Literally, my dad shook me awake. He barreled into my room one morning before he left for work and made it clear that sleeping in all day was not an option. He said something to the effect of, "What is your plan for the day? You gotta have a plan for the day!" In my mind, I was thinking, *Jiminy Christmas, I plan to shoot hoops, maybe play some golf, drink some beer, go see Jodi!*

Those who know Dad will completely relate to Coach Billman's presence. His is hard to articulate. I never thought of my dad as mean or nasty for the sake of it. He had a special way of motivating teams, whether on the football field or in the office. His motivation was and always has been of the "you-can-do-better" variety. We all need somebody who cares about us enough to help us to reach our God-given potential. Truth be known, many of us, myself included, run on 50 percent of our actual capacity. My dad and my coaches have always pushed me to work harder and tap into my physical and mental capabilities.

For a spell, I resented him for waking me up, mostly because of my earning a full scholarship and working every summer in between. In my

> We all need somebody who cares about us enough to help us to reach our God-given potential.

young adult mind, I had worked hard, played five seasons of football, earned my degree, and deserved a little bit of "me time." My dad was right, of course, in that the world waits for nobody. In other words, if you as a human being aren't constantly moving forward in a positive way, the world will move on without you. You are either moving backward or forward. You can't stay in one place for very long. It is a great lesson for all of us to remember. So when your parents, grandparents, coaches, a boss, or a partner are pushing you, it means they care and see great potential in you. Too often, we can feel sorry for ourselves, which is a waste. The only useful response to life is to get better and try harder.

After recovering from the cold cup of coffee (that is my dad), I woke up and got moving. I got off my butt and went out to make a connection at Worthington

Industries, a well-known and extremely respected public steel company based in Columbus. I had a good connection through Bob Messaros, who had been a coach at Miami and recruited me to the football program. After leaving a successful coaching career, he had gone to work with Worthington. The door opened for an interview with a mountain of a man, Ike Kelly, who played for *the* Ohio State Buckeyes and then in the NFL for the Philadelphia Eagles. I have big hands, but my hand disappeared when shaking his massive hand.

> Too often, we can feel sorry for ourselves, which is a waste. The only useful response to life is to get better and try harder.

With the economy a bit soft at the time, Worthington Steel was not hiring. Persistence became the way, and I basically begged for a job from Ike. He was the vice president of human resources, and nobody got hired without going through him. John McConnell, the founder of Worthington and a former navy veteran and college football player at Michigan State University, believed in hiring athletes. In the early days, it was mostly Ohio State football players, but over time the company grew and began to diversify its hiring, tapping former athletes from different schools. McConnell was famous for saying that if he hired college athletes, if he hired competitive people who worked hard and played as a team, his company would find success. His simple yet effective formula was to hire winners.

I was not a winner that day. Ike's response was roughly, "You look like a nice young man, but we just aren't hiring." While driving home, I prepared myself to face Dad. I love my dad, but he is an intimidating guy. Think marine, successful football coach, driven business leader. Not scary, but focused and intense.

"How'd the interview go?" Dad asked. I told him. "What else do you have?" was his next question. Not wanting to go through this each day, my competitive spirit kicked in, as it does when I have my mind set on something. *It's go time. I will earn that starting position.*

I started my campaign by turning my attention back to Ike Kelly. Using a combination of calls, emails, and in-person begging, I ultimately wore the man down. In February 1991, a couple of months after I graduated from college, he offered me a job in the steel plant. I didn't even ask what they would pay me, but I believe it ended up being around $17,000 per year.

Despite doing what he told me to do, Dad was not impressed. "You have a degree, and you're going to work in a steel plant?" My higher education, of course, did not line up with working in the plant.

From Worthington's perspective, they tested young college grads in the plant before actually bringing them inside and hiring them in sales. During my training program, I worked hard alongside the production guys and earned their respect. In Andy Billman style, I cut my nose on a slitting line but kept working after getting stitched up. I did not want the guys to see me as a wimp. Yet another example that showcases both my clumsiness and my drive.

I learned so much in that six-month training program, and the most important part was coming to understand who actually makes the money for the company. The men and women I was lucky enough to work alongside were the real heroes. I used that early experience to cement my thinking and garner true respect for anyone who directly helps make or deliver a product or service to customers.

Even today, I always try to remember to tell the folks making the money for the company that I am overhead and do my best to authentically let those individuals know how important they are to the company.

Pause for Reflection: Opportunity

What are some of the wake-up calls you have received in your life? If needed, how might you create a wake-up call for yourself right now?

Occasionally opportunities are masked as something you are not initially attracted to. Are there opportunities you have passed by because they didn't match what you had in mind?

Who has motivated you to move forward from a setback or to try something new in your life?

> Are you willing to take a personal risk to try something new?

Are you willing to take a personal risk to try something new? If not, what is holding you back?

POSTSEASON
CAREER, FAMILY, AND LOSS

*Our greatest glory is not in never falling
but in rising every time we fall.*
—Oliver Goldsmith

CHAPTER 7

BELTS AND SUSPENDERS IN THE BULLPEN AND MARRIAGE

*Life is inherently risky. There is only one
big risk you should avoid at all costs, and
that is the risk of doing nothing.*
—Denis Waitley

Flash Forward: Ugh! My feet feel like they are going to fall off. I don't think my legs can keep moving. My chest hurts with every breath I take. I think I might have a heart attack. I'm not even halfway done. I want to stop. I can't do this. How am I going to finish? Why did my buddy talk me into running a marathon? What was I thinking? This is the hardest thing I've ever had to do. I just want to quit. I don't think I can finish this.

Stop it! Don't think like that. I've spent several grueling, tough months filled with blood, sweat, and tears training for this. I can't quit. I just can't. I have to push through.

I have to prove to myself that I can do more than I think I can do. My body is about to fall apart, but I will remain mentally strong. I can do this. I can do this. Don't stop. Don't give up. Keep going, Andy! You will cross the finish line. You will finish!

Jodi and I got engaged shortly before I graduated from college and married soon after graduation. In retrospect, it was a bit quick. As I reflect on that decision and time, I have absolutely no regrets at all. I have always been a guy who is very comfortable pushing the quick start on just about any big decision in my life.

When you're young and in love, one thing you may not have is an abundance of cash. Buying the rings took planning. It didn't help that I lost my ring—twice. Let me tell you about the first wedding ring. For our honeymoon, we went on a cruise. We met a couple from Indiana and had a great time. While visiting them later at a lake house, can you guess what I did? I lost my wedding ring in the lake when it slipped off my finger. Sometime later, when Jodi and I were living in a small apartment, we were robbed, and I lost wedding ring number two! Some people would consider two lost rings as a bad omen. Not us. We were and are in it through thick and thin, in good times and bad, wedding ring or no wedding ring.

Newlywed and fresh out of college, I took a sales position with Worthington Industries in Columbus. The thick competition on the sales team was reminiscent of a bunch of competitive athletes in a bullpen. We were all eagerly awaiting the next opportunity. Of course, an "Andy moment" would occur, and luckily it did not derail my chances of getting that next, better job. In trying to impress the older guys, I wore a pair of pants with suspenders and a belt. Yes, you read that correctly—suspenders and a belt, at the same time. Everybody—except me at that time in my life—knew that you did not wear suspenders with a belt.

The whole thing is a little ironic because "belts and suspenders" is an idiom for minimizing risk. It originated in the banking industry and referred to bankers demanding strict adherence to loan policies. When taken literally, wearing both is a cautionary procedure, adding backup or multiple layers of safety. For those wondering, Google says it is a fashion mistake. But I am a risk-taker and typically a calculated risk-taker. I do not always put on my "belt and suspenders" when going after my next goal, but occasionally I do. Most of the time, I set my sights and charge forward. I say yes to opportunities then drive forward with tenacity.

> Say yes to opportunities, then drive forward with tenacity.

I love these words from Dean Alfange's "My Creed": "I do not choose to be a common man. It is my right to be uncommon if I can. I seek opportunity, not security. I want to take the calculated risk: to dream and to build, to fail and to succeed. To think and act for myself and to face the world boldly and say: This I have done."

Belts and suspenders fashion mistakes aside, this was a time of learning and growth for me. I was all-in on my new career, and from 1991 to 1993, I worked hard and set my target on a promotion to a position in outside sales. Finally, I received an offer to go on the road. It was definitely a big say-yes moment for me. Things moved quickly; I got a company car, was assigned a territory in Michigan and a lone customer up in Sault Ste. Marie, Ontario, Canada. With a little help from my dad, Jodi and I scraped up enough money for a down payment on our first home in Grand Blanc, Michigan. It was time to leave Columbus.

Inside Worthington's commission program, it takes time to build the business and open doors for more connections. As hard as it was for me to gain real traction, the company was right to make sure I had what it took to be in sales. What better way to focused dedication than with a program designed with enticing incentives? In my first year on the road in my new position, Jodi and I used the pop can refund money to buy a pizza on a Friday night while I waited for a commission check the following week. But we were *happy*, and our struggles were a good reminder that money does not make us happier, nor does our zip code. You must choose to be happy.

During this transition, I was twenty-five, and Jodi was twenty-four and pregnant with our first child, Ellie Marie. Jodi has always been the stronger one in our marriage, and she took on this move like a champ. We were hours from home and did not know one person in the state of Michigan. I spent more time on the road and committed to the grind more than ever. As for Jodi, she went from working in medical billing to working for a private aviation firm. She knew when we got married that Worthington had a culture of moving people around a lot, and she also knew it was a dream of mine to get an outside sales job and proceed to move up within the company. I have never been comfortable unless I am uncomfortable, growing, and moving forward. I guess I have some of my dad in me, after all!

Michigan turned out to be a transformative period in our lives. We had four kids and built amazing relationships. It was during this time our faith journey together began with an invitation to Bible Study Fellowship from our neighbors, Jim and Cinda Rachor. Jodi encouraged me to accept the invitation as I was initially reluctant. By reluctant, I mean I did the "holy Heisman" move.

The BSF program is a non-denominational structured Bible study, with separate sessions for men and women, held once a week. Can you guess what happened next? No, I did not do something that resulted in a visit to an emergency room, but I did jump from being inactive in the church to a BSF leader. *Go figure.* The Rachors adopted us in faith, and we began attending a Presbyterian church. It turned out to be such a wonderful time of growth.

Baby Ryan came along in March 1996, with Baby Emily following just two years later in January 1998. During that time, I accepted a promotion to be the General Motors account manager. This was a high-profile opportunity among the sales group, a big piece of business for the company. Another bit of irony was my connection to the person I was now working for, Bob Messaros. He had recruited me to play at Miami, later introduced me to Worthington, and ultimately became my direct boss. It was a great opportunity to finally play for Bob, albeit on a different field, so to speak. With our growing family and budget, it was time to move into a larger house. We relocated to Davison, Michigan, which was not too far from Grand Blanc. And last but not least, in February 2000, Baby Owen completed our family of six. To this day, we sometimes still call him the caboose of the family.

You never know where a yes will lead. Move forward with anticipation and make time for what matters. Even during times of transformation, there is time to build relationships, practice your faith, nurture your family, and grow personally and professionally.

You never know where a yes will lead. Move forward with anticipation and make time for what matters.

Entrepreneur's Creed

I do not choose to be a common man.
It is my right to be uncommon if I can.
I seek opportunity, not security.
I do not wish to be a kept citizen,
Humbled and dulled by having
the State look after me.
I want to take the calculated risk,
To dream and to build. To fail and to succeed.
I refuse to barter incentive for a dole;
I prefer the challenges of life to
the guaranteed existence;
The thrill of fulfillment to the stale calm of Utopia.
I will not trade freedom for beneficence
Nor my dignity for a handout
I will never cower before any master
Nor bend to any threat.
It is my heritage to stand erect, proud, and unafraid;
To think and act for myself,
To enjoy the benefit of my creations
And to face the world boldly and say:
This, with God's help, I have done.
All this is what it means to be an Entrepreneur.
(International Entrepreneurs Association,
adapted from Dean Alfange's "My Creed")

Pause for Reflection: Calculated Risk

Sometimes we have to say yes even when others around us are saying no or wait.

If you have a new opportunity that possibly includes a physical move for you and or your family, remember: "Happiness isn't a zip code."

Most of us, myself included at times, do everything we can to avoid any personal or professional risk. Of course, it is always good to seek input from people you trust before making a big move in life, but don't forget to follow your own heart and intuition when taking a risk.

> Seek input from people you trust before making a big move in life, but don't forget to follow your own heart and intuition when taking a risk.

When and where have been your times of growth? How about times when the thought of risk might have been holding back your growth?

What invitations have you accepted or declined and why?

CHAPTER 8
THE FAILED INTERVIEW AND BUYER'S REMORSE

Most people have uphill dreams but downhill habits. You have to intentionally turn downhill sliding into uphill climbing.
—John C. Maxwell

Flash Forward. I've made it through another day of treatment. As I slowly walk to the bedroom to get ready for bed, I realize I feel shitty. I brush my teeth, change clothes, and head to the bathroom to take my chemo pills. It's only Day 4, and I'm already feeling the side effects. The doctors and nurses told me what to expect from the chemo, but the headache, the nausea . . . it's no joke. For a split second, I look at the pills in my hand, hesitating to swallow them. I take a deep breath and remind myself this process is a marathon, not a sprint. I know I need to suck it up and leave the rest to God. I have no choice. I need to finish the race. I pop the pills, lie my head on the pillow, and decide I will wake up and live tomorrow the best way I know how.

After about a year of being on the road in Michigan and handling bigger accounts, an East Coast sales manager position became available. I was hungry for growth, so I leaned into the opportunity with my manager and made it known to Worthington's president that I wanted the job. Despite my eagerness and overconfidence, I did not get the job. It stung a bit because I thought I deserved it and was a natural fit. Things happen for a reason, though, right?

About three weeks after losing out on the opportunity to go east, I bumped into someone in the airport. This was a customer I had worked with and sold steel to when I first started in outside sales and before I took the key account position. My approach was to treat every customer like they were my only customer, and we had a good relationship. He happened to be the owner and had his sales guy with him. We had a brief conversation that day, followed later by another meetup. One thing led to another, and I eventually became the vice president of sales with their company, A.M.S.E.A.

Worthington tried to keep me on. My manager invited me on a little road trip to meet with the president. In those days, fewer people job-hopped. Fewer still would have left a great company like Worthington. The president did his very best to talk me out of leaving, reassuring me that there would be a bigger and better opportunity down the road. He encouraged me to be patient, but I said I had to do this thing and give it a try. Looking back, it was such a great life lesson: You do not always get what you want, and that's a good thing!

You do not always get what you want, and that's a good thing!

I often wonder what would have happened had I not voluntarily left Worthington Industries. How would the trajectory of my career have played out? Would future opportunities have come my way? Or did taking the risk and learning how to do things differently help me become a better leader for future roles? What I do know is that *not* getting that job served as a catalyst for joining another team—a team I said yes to.

The position was in Flint, Michigan, which had one of the highest murder rates in the nation at the time. It turned out to be a very hard and initially awkward adjustment. I felt a serious pang of buyer's remorse, as in, *what did I just do?* I left a multi-billion-dollar, publicly held organization with great benefits, pay, and brand recognition for a small eighteen-million-dollar revenue, privately-held, eighty-five-person, two-factory plant company. The majority owner and founder wanted to grow the company, and I assumed at the time he wanted to bring in a catalyst (me) to help them grow.

He already had a vice president of sales, so he positioned me as a vice president of sales and marketing, creating an inevitable conflict. My role was in new business development. The vice president of sales and vice president of operations did not exactly welcome me to the company. I could not blame them. They were both the de facto day-to-day leaders of the business. I completely understood their initial resistance. I don't believe the owner had socialized the concept of me coming into the company that much. To make things more difficult, this team was a former customer when I first came to Michigan. Another great lesson for me to catalog for the future—any time you are thinking about bringing in a new leader to your company, take the time to make sure everyone knows the new person's role.

Not only did I put myself to the test in professional growth that year, but I challenged myself physically as well by running a marathon in Chicago. My best friend from childhood and fraternity brother at Miami, Ryan O'Dell, encouraged me to run the race. It turned out to be the hardest physical feat I had ever attempted, and that includes playing college football. I had previously run a half-marathon with my brother in Michigan, but it was nothing compared to the full race. Jodi, as usual, supported my desire to try something new and difficult, however crazy it was. I trained hard, going out every weekend to put in more miles. The demands of training required hours of my time—time I should have been at home helping with the kids. I finished in five hours and twenty minutes and some change with a pace of twelve minutes and thirteen seconds per mile and placed 25,798[th] of 28,830 total finishers, but at least I wasn't last!

A little old lady sporting blue hair passed me. Several times during the race, I wanted to quit and sneak off into an alley and take a cab to the finish line. But I could hear Mom and Dad's voices in the background pushing me forward. We were not a family that quit anything, and their early training to finish what you start, no matter the result, kept me on the path.

Preparing for that race and staying on course was yet another challenge in my life, another hard thing I persevered through that psychologically prepared me for the marathon of battling brain cancer. It might have been harder on me in the moment because I needed a hip replacement at age forty. But pushing through the pain and completing the race was worth it and only made me stronger. If brain cancer eventually takes me down, let us just say it will not be without a fight! Regardless of the outcome, whether a marathon, career obstacle, relationship detour, or health challenge, persevering through the difficult time and coming out on the other side just might be its own reward.

Pause for Reflection: Personal Development

When you don't get what you want, it may be because something better is waiting for you or a different lesson is there for you to learn. Look for the silver linings and nuggets of learning along the way.

Something better is waiting for you.

What happens when you get buyer's remorse? Commit to success on your new path. Have you ever had a career type of buyer's remorse? How did you persevere and grow?

And what about when it comes to finishing a race you are currently running, whether this is a project you need to finish, a medical circumstance you are battling, life itself, or some other adversity? How do you set yourself up to finish?

For me, I need to show up, do what the doctors say, take the drugs—including the ones that I detest because they make me feel awful and cause my face to swell. I can't just opt out or quit. Even when I feel horrible, I have to keep going. I wake up, put one foot in front of the other, and live my life.

How will you finish your race?

CHAPTER 9
FROM LOSING IT ALL
TO A GOD THING

*In life, the challenge is not so much to figure
out how best to play the game; the challenge is
to figure out what game you're playing.*
—Kwame Appiah

Flash Forward: It's strange to think this is becoming habit—part of my daily routine. Today, Jodi (sometimes it's my brother) drops me off at the main entrance and goes to the park as I walk in for my treatment. I look at my watch. Perfect timing. It's 7:30 a.m. My radiation appointment is at 8:00 a.m. sharp. I can't help but think of my dad who always said, "If you're five minutes early, you're late!"

I make my way to the radiation wing and notice the big doors are closed and locked, which is very unusual. With a big sigh of frustration, I think to myself, **You've got to be** *kidding me. I don't have time for this.* I look at my watch about every minute. *What is going on?*

Finally, at 8:07 a.m., with my impatience getting the best of me, a young radiation tech with a smile on her face opens the door to the radiation treatment unit, "Good morning, how are you?" Without thinking, I blurt out, "Not good . . . have a major problem . . . brain cancer . . . we're late. We're here to beat cancer. We can't be late if we're gonna beat cancer." The minute those words leave my lips, I feel bad. I just made a big deal out of this minor thing in front of everyone. Poor girl.

Quickly realizing I was a little out of line, I gather my thoughts, take a deep breath, and restate my comments in a much friendlier tone, "I have places to be and a team counting on me, and you have other patients that need your team to be on time EVERY day! Let's not be late again." I think it's fair to say, they know how serious I am about attacking this tumor.

As I walk out the same doors that frustrated me moments earlier, knowing I'm running late to get to work, I quickly aim to clear my head of the internal chatter, *Am I going to be okay? Get through this? Die?* Instead of allowing these thoughts to overwhelm me, I focus on being the first to work. It's my way of turning my situation into a game. A contest. I must push myself, stay active and competitive. I need to feel alive.

In 2002, I became plant manager at A.M.S.E.A. and forced myself to try something functionally different from what I knew. The company owner encouraged me along the way, reminding me that if I ever wanted to own the company, the best way to get there would be to learn everything about it, not only sales. It was a hard, hard job, but I learned a ton about the work and myself. That lesson taught me never to underestimate how hard you might think someone else's job is or is not. This experience truly opened my eyes.

After just a couple of short years in the role, the CFO wanted to retire, which led to the president and majority owner offering me the opportunity to buy out his partner. The CFO had started the company alongside the owner and had decided to enjoy his much-earned retirement. After getting some help from an attorney and a lot of back-and-forth negotiation, I entered into a stock purchase agreement with him to buy his approximate 25 percent ownership stake in the company.

At the age of thirty-six and with four kids, I did not have the cash to fund the entire purchase price, so I took out a personal loan from the company's local bank for hundreds of thousands of dollars and scraped together an additional $20,000 up-front for the down payment. We structured the deal in a way that allowed me to make the interest payment to the bank while increasing my salary to support the loan. The third component of the deal was to utilize the excess cash flow of the business to pay the CFO out completely eventually. My loan from the bank included a personal guarantee, meaning the company does not back it. When people ask where I got my MBA, my stock answer has been, "From the School of Hard Knocks!"

In 2005, I became vice president of operations, and we moved the company from Michigan to Tennessee on the eastern side of the state. Jodi stayed with the kids while I moved to Tennessee to set up the new plant alongside my partner. The plan was for the family to follow soon after. In the meantime, I lived with two other guys who were a part of our team in an older home. I remember sleeping on a mattress without a frame that sat directly on the floor. This was another incredibly difficult time in my life.

Jodi was very skeptical at this stage of the business arrangement. Her intuition has always been stronger than mine, and to be honest, I was incredibly lonely during this time. I felt like I was a part of the exodus in biblical times, like an Israelite wandering in the wilderness. At least every other weekend, I traveled back and forth, but it just was not the same. I know many families have situations where the parents travel a lot and are not home every weekend. I respect anybody who structures their business and family lives as such, but I realized it was not for me. Some people enjoy the quiet time or are a lot more comfortable being away, but not me. Although I would not exactly call myself a socialite, I prefer to be around my wife and family.

As 2005 ended and 2006 began, a massive setback—a losing season—closed in on me. A situation somewhat out of my control plunged me into the midst of a legal battle. With business and contractual language and words such as covenants, forbearance, and lawsuits, let us just say I was on a fast-track education on these legal terms and processes. If I knew then what I know now, I would have challenged the terms or paid more attention to the what-if scenarios. I had adequate representation, but I failed to ask the right questions about what would happen in the event of a downside scenario. In the summer of 2006, I worked toward resolving the legal issues, and the company ultimately paid back the open balance owed to the bank from the original loan.

Here I was, age thirty-eight and losing it all. Through all of this, Jodi stood behind me. My friends and my family prayed over me for a solution to this awful situation. The embarrassment and the sense of failure were almost too great to bear until I had an undeniable God moment. It was, in every way, a rescue. We came to a confidential settlement. I will never forget driving directly to the bank—in a cold sweat and gripping the wheel to control the shaking—to pay back the commercial loan. This money to buy out the former CFO mostly came from a bank loan. I still owed $25,000, and Jodi and I did not have it. I learned that I had a tax refund from the company that matched the settlement figure exactly. It was a gift from God, I am sure of it.

In the midst of leaving that company in 2006, I received the opportunity to return to Worthington Industries to manage national accounts, which would allow me to transition back to stability, spend time with Jodi and the kids, and rebuild my career. This was another God wink, another call. I said yes and made the best of this time and my position back at Worthington. With the support of the company and the help of my great team, I enjoyed success and was able to open up doors to some big customers we had never sold to before. I felt like I had rebounded and that another setback had turned into a comeback!

Doing well in this new capacity at Worthington set me up for an opportunity to head a sales region out East, leading eight outside sales reps and teaming up with a great operations manager of a steel processing facility based in Baltimore, Maryland, and Rock Hill, South Carolina. Although this was a fantastic opportunity for my professional career, I soon realized that 2007 and 2008 was a terrible time to try to sell a house. Nevertheless, I naively accepted the opportunity, even though it came at such an inopportune time and carried great personal financial risk. To take the position, we were required to move out East to be near the business I was leading. Once again, I dragged Jodi along for another new opportunity. I said yes, and despite the personal difficulties, away we went.

One of my bigger setbacks appeared to be the depreciation of our home, and despite the recession, we decided to sell and move on to the next big opportunity. The personal sacrifice did not come without pain, and the company did everything they could to help us get moved and work through the bad timing in the market. This was a poor decision on my part. When it came time to buy a new home in Raleigh, North Carolina (located near my sister-in-law), with the poor state of the financial market, we were not in a good enough position to buy a new home, so we moved into a rental home. We also enrolled the kids in public school for the first time. I saw it all as a chance to move up professionally and hit reset.

This all turned out to be a rocky period of adjustment for our family. I began traveling four to five days per week. Our children had an ever-present mom and a quasi-absentee dad. This was a game-changing time in my career that resulted in exposure to senior management back at the head office in Columbus. I do not regret the decision to say yes to the opportunity, but it made me more thoughtful about my family's impact going forward.

During all this transition, I got a hip replacement at age forty. It was one of the best decisions I have ever made. I learned that I was predisposed to have the procedure based on how my body developed from a young age. Playing college football and running a marathon did not help, of course. Health challenges can be tricky because they can be so debilitating.

This chapter in my life, when I took job opportunities I thought were best but in hindsight put my family in distress, was an absolute disaster and showcased an embarrassing and vulnerable part of my life. To this day, I hold on to these yes moments as yet more opportunities for me to learn and grow as a young business leader. Had I not taken these chances, I would not have earned the opportunity to be hired as the vice president of purchasing for the entire company. Though painstaking and humbling at times, it was absolutely a catalyst for my career.

You never know when one door closes what other doors might open. Put another way, if you do not ever take personal risks, how will you ever grow? I encourage you to lean into new and different experiences that challenge you at your core. Accepting these stretch opportunities has helped me understand myself, what I am good at, and what I like to do. When you are ready to give up, hold out and lean in.

You never know where the next opportunity or blessing will come from. You do not have to let the bad things take you down. Use them as your motivation to push through.

> When you are ready to give up, hold out and lean in. You never know where the next opportunity or blessing will come from.

Pause for Reflection: Consequential Learning

Look in your rearview mirror at an important decision. What did you like about it? What didn't you like? How did it help you grow? How will the outcome shape a future decision?

Look ahead and think it through when you are weighing an important decision.

Have you ever had one of the moments or experiences (like me living in an old house with a few other guys away from my family) when you think, *What the hell am I doing?*

Brain cancer continues to teach me a valuable lesson. No matter your circumstance or situation, if you look deeply enough, you will find rich blessings. By slowing down, exercising patience, then reframing your perspective and looking at your trials and tribulations through a new lens, you will find new wisdom and strength for your future.

Remember when I told you about fast walking from my radiation treatments to work? I turned my obstacle into a game.

> No matter your circumstance or situation, if you look deeply enough, you will find rich blessings.

What setback are you currently experiencing?

How will you come back from it?

How can you turn your trial into a little game to pass the time or, better yet, improve your health and mindset along the way?

CHAPTER 10

FROM PROMOTED TO VP TO 'STEP ASIDE, BILLMAN'

*The successful man lengthens his stride when
he discovers that the signpost has deceived him;
the failure looks for a place to sit down.*
—J.R. Rogers

Flash Forward: As I sit with my wife in the waiting room for my first round of radiation, I feel my heart beating out of my chest, as I don't fully know what to expect. As I breathe and try to distract myself from the overwhelming anxiety and show my wife I'm okay, I notice a ninety-year-old woman waiting for her turn. As I begin to wonder what her situation is, I hear my name, "Andrew Billman." I look at my wife, grab her hand, muster a confident smile, and then follow the nurse into the radiation room.

Before I have a chance to acclimate to this unfamiliar experience, the nurses ask me to lie down on the table.

Once I do, they gently position my limbs and then CLAMP. CLAMP. CLAMP. CLAMP. They just physically constrained me to this table. This is it. There is no going back. I don't know if I can do this. My whole body feels like it's shaking and sweating as the technician approaches with **the mask**. I see the bright lights dimming as she lowers the mask to my face. I'm trying hard not to panic, but all I can think about is how claustrophobic I felt when they fit me for the mask. SNAP. SNAP. SNAP. SNAP. The touch of the mask is cool yet so snug. I want it off. **Breathe**, I keep telling myself. **There are holes in the mask. You can do this. Just breathe.** As traumatized as I feel right now, if that ninety-year-old woman can endure radiation treatment, so can I. **Andy, you've got this. Just do it.**

In January 2010, I received another life-changing opportunity. I was sitting on the porch with Jodi at our rental home in North Carolina. We had not bought a house yet because we had lost all our equity from our last home in Michigan. In the meantime, we had been saving and getting to know the area. We felt like we were ready. The next day an unexpected call came in from Worthington Industries: "Andy, we'd like to interview you. Come on up." I did not have to convince Jodi of whether or not to consider. Getting back home to Ohio was a welcoming idea, and the opportunity to work for Worthington Industries again had me excited.

The COO at the time took me to lunch and, after a series of questions, asked the big one: "Andy, all I need to know is if I offer you this job, with no other details, will you say yes?"

You know what I said. Right on the spot, I said yes without knowing the salary or benefits because I did not care about the money. It was a trust question. He wanted to see if my motivations aligned and if I was in it for the right reasons. I'm wired to say yes to new opportunities, but my former boss taught me a great lesson that day.

I knew the offer had to be another one of those God moments, a part of his orchestration. Why would they want to interview me for the vice president of purchasing position when almost all my functional experience had been in sales? They credited my prior private experience with the company up in Michigan, where I was in charge of purchasing and operations, though it was on a significantly smaller scale. Regardless of how unlikely it seemed, the job offered our family the chance to move back *home* after seventeen years. It was a chance to recover from our financial mess in Michigan, followed by our move to North Carolina. The job also provided me exposure to the board of directors, which would later prove valuable.

After I was promoted to vice president of purchasing at Worthington Industries, I started out traveling back and forth from Raleigh-Durham to Columbus until the kids finished school. Then, in July, we bought a house. Jodi had given me the dreaded job of finding a home on my own. Every day after work, I ran around with a realtor. By the way, I do not know about *you* when it comes to house hunting, but for me, it was punishment. Every house and neighborhood started to look the same, but I was happy to endure the process if it meant bringing us all back together.

As I settled into my new purchasing role and got the family situated, I did my very best to influence the company culture positively. At first, as you could imagine, coming from spending most of my career in sales, I wasn't exactly welcomed by the purchasing group, nor was I given a manual for what they expected of me. The sink-or-swim culture we had at the time was perfect for me, and I sincerely appreciated the autonomy to go about the job the way I felt best.

After meeting the existing team, which included more than twenty-five colleagues, I understood who did what and started developing a strategy that would bring a positive result to the bottom line. At the end of the day, my job was to bring savings to the company while protecting our reputation in the marketplace. My role in purchasing was to ensure that my team was supporting the sales professionals who were working hard to grow the company.

What I learned in the early days was that we had the raw ingredients to be successful. I inherited a very capable team and helped to acquire a few new ones along the way. The biggest issue I identified was that we were not close enough to the market and the sales team we were supposed to support. As I sought to move things ahead, I learned a valuable lesson about how to invert my thinking about the best method to inspire our purchasing team to buy into my strategy.

Using the experience of being a former sales leader, I simply encouraged our bright purchasing group to think like and act like sales professionals. This required our purchasing leaders to get on the phones with the customers and our sales teams, find creative ways to help the customer, and ultimately bring the orders our way. Within a few short months, we had our entire purchasing team turned around and focused on helping to grow the business.

We set into motion the Flywheel Effect that Jim Collins articulated in his *Good to Great* books. By drastically speeding up our response time and getting closer to the purchasers within our customer base, we earned more business and created more purchasing volume for our team to negotiate with from our many supply partners. This was counterintuitive for many, but our team became very market and sales focused over a short period.

I encouraged our team to get inside the market and travel with our sales teams, play golf with and go to lunch with our customers, and capitalize on every opportunity to build relationships authentically. We were able to get everyone to understand that we only had an opportunity to buy something when our sales professionals sold something. It sounds obvious, but sales departments don't exactly sync with the purchasing group in many organizations.

My short experience leading a purchasing team opened the door for another say-yes moment in my career. In 2011, this opportunity came in the form of an offer to be the next president of Worthington Cylinders—a wholly owned subsidiary of Worthington Industries—when the current president decided to retire. While it was a massive opportunity for a young guy to grow the business, it was also a huge personal and professional risk.

We say yes every day—to phone calls, meetings, and emails. These are small yeses. In life, we also have the big yeses, the life-changing yeses, the yeses that bring both risk and reward, learning and growth. I highly recommend seeking wise counsel when a major opportunity presents itself, and you are weighing a big yes or no. This particular yes was nothing short of risk. It was well out of my comfort zone and a huge stretch. It would again challenge me to my core. But as I've said before, I am not comfortable unless I am uncomfortable.

I said yes to that opportunity, the company's board of directors completed its consideration of other candidates, and I got the nod to be the next president. I inherited a cash-cow business, and although the company had been consistently successful over the past forty or so years, the board was hungry to bring in a catalyst, someone who could grow the company and open up new markets.

When I was installed, I also inherited the existing management team. Something inherent within me is that I am loyal. In this case, as would be later viewed by leadership, I am loyal to a fault. Instead of shaking things up or considering bringing in a new team, I chose to lean into the current leadership team and bet on my ability to influence the change I desired and that the board expected. I naively learned through this opportunity that some of the team members had a stronghold in the past, holding us back a bit. I should have pushed harder to affect the real change we desired.

Nevertheless, I worked with our team, and we doubled the revenue, taking Worthington Cylinders from about $500 million to $1 billion in sales, a new high, while opening up many new avenues of growth, mostly through an aggressive acquisition strategy. Though we were steadily growing, in January 2016, I found myself facing what I thought to be the most *earth-shattering* setback of my career. I was asked to step aside from the president role. When I reflect on that time now, I own my choices and acknowledge that we were not prepared for the rapid growth we experienced and had certainly hit some speed bumps along the way. The COO who hired me for both the vice president of purchasing and the president of cylinders positions had retired. The new COO wanted to restructure the business.

They gave me plenty of time to consider staying with the company and offered to work with me to identify a new role where I might continue to be useful. Most companies do not offer a second chance, but Worthington, being the special type of company that it is, respected what we had done over the last four years and wanted to offer a soft landing. I was grateful for the thoughtfulness but knew immediately that it was time for me to move on. I decided to get out of the COO's way by the end of the meeting in which I received the news. I saw this change much the way you see it happen with head coaches. In that setting, there can only be one head coach. When the senior leadership of a company or owners of a professional team want to make a change, it is time to hand over the whistle to the next leader.

A big part of my decision to leave was grounded in my respect for the company and the team I had helped grow. I believed the best path for me was to step aside and move on with grace and dignity—to take the high road. But, in all honesty, it wasn't that simple, and I was completely devastated by the change. I had experienced other setbacks in my life, but the magnitude of this one was particularly difficult to swallow. After having such a great recovery after my experience at the private manufacturing company, this one just stung in a different way. I will never forget coming home after that meeting. Jodi, with an intuition that has always amazed me, immediately asked me what was wrong. I told her what had happened and that I decided to move on as quickly as possible. She supported my decision 100 percent and was quick to remind me that "we'd be fine," just like my mom had always told me.

It took some time, but after absorbing the change and finding proper perspective, I realized I was much more comfortable leading on a smaller scale. How will you find your true north unless you say yes to moving away from your comfort zone? It is a calibration of sorts. If you do well in your job or career, you will likely be promoted within your organization. You will continue to progress until you reach your ceiling of potential in that particular role. Being introspective along the way is key to avoiding frustration, burnout, or in my case, an unplanned exit.

Regardless of how my tenure as president concluded, my aim has always been to reach my God-given potential. When we find ourselves in a role that may not be the best fit, we can still learn and develop. Where people go wrong is when they see this ceiling as a failure.

Bringing in a bit of my dad's wisdom from his thoughts that he added to quotes he shared with us from a young age, "When your best plans fail, get at the problem. Don't whimper and feel sorry for your mistakes. Obstacles are just more challenges to your character. You will not be without obstacles. How you face them is the real issue!"

Pause for Reflection: Perspective

Our immediate response to being asked to step aside from anything brings a feeling of defeat, anger, embarrassment, pity, and all kinds of other negative thoughts. To move past that overarching feeling of failure, we must exchange our fear for hope and embrace growth, learning, and gratitude.

Use the setback to lean into what happened and start thinking about your next move. Use the setback as motivation to develop a new path to create your comeback.

Use the setback as motivation to develop a new path to create your comeback.

Harness the power of perspective when bad things happen to you. It is completely normal to feel down or to question why something happened to you. You might never know the answer, but let yourself process all of your feelings, own what happened, and move past it to create a new future.

OFF-SEASON
HEALTH BATTLE INTO FAITH, WISDOM, AND TEACHING

If you can't fly, then run; if you can't run, then
walk; if you can't walk, then crawl; but whatever
you do, you have to keep moving forward.
—Martin Luther King Jr.

CHAPTER 11

A SEASON TO SEARCH, REENERGIZE, FIND PEACE AND NEW PURPOSE

Have you ever thought about just being there with your family?
—An RPN at Ohio State University
Wexner Medical Center

Flash Forward: Here I am, sitting in the same examining room I've been in so many times before, back for yet another checkup. Same posters on the wall. Same smell that I can't explain. Same friendly, caring nurses checking my vitals. Right as I begin to wonder how long I'll wait this time, in walks the nurse. "Hi, Andy! How are you?" "I'm doing great! I'm busy getting ready for a business trip." Before I can even continue, this sweet nurse interrupts me with a look of concern and slight annoyance and says again, "No, Andy. What I mean is, how are **you** doing?"

At this moment, a light begins to go off in my conscience as I realize she doesn't care about my business trip. Instead, she wants to know how I am handling having malignant brain cancer and how I am choosing to prioritize and reorganize my life to adapt to this huge life change. What she is doing for me is slapping me in the face to wake me up to the reality I'm living. "Have you stopped to think about what's best for you and your family during this time?"

I don't know what to say in response because she's right. I've been so caught up in continuing life that I haven't stopped to reflect on what's best for my family and me at this moment while I'm fighting for my life. She put me in a time-out—one I so desperately needed but hadn't fully realized until now. As she takes my blood pressure, I sit in deep thought, grateful that this insightful woman knew what I needed to hear. Things are going to change. It's time to focus on my family and me.

After moving on from Worthington, I took some time to rest, soul search, and honor myself and my family before taking on my next challenge. From family trips to Italy, Utah, and Florida to see my dad to reading, exercising, and networking, my objective during that time was to rest, reset, and refocus on the things that mattered most to me. Stepping away from the day-to-day business grind, the grind that comes with a high-stress role, was a blessing in disguise. I especially savored the ski trip out to Utah with Jodi and the kids because I did not have the stress of getting back to work. I had some worry for the future, of course, but I used that time to decompress.

Back at home, I accepted some paid consulting roles by phone and in-person for local businesses. I did keep a pole in the water for corporate-level opportunities but mostly had opportunities from out of town. Jodi supported me in taking a job out of town but made it clear she was not moving again. After all that had happened and moving around multiple times, I felt it was time to honor what she wanted. Although I looked at some businesses to buy personally, I did not immediately find anything. So I exercised great patience in not chasing the next big opportunity and decided just to let God do his thing.

During that time of reflection from February to December 2016, I spent many a day still in shock. No one had ever asked me to move aside in my entire life, nor had I ever been out of work my entire life. The entire situation reminded me of the adage that warns never to put your identity in something you can lose, so I focused on doing more around the house—short of making a meal because I cannot cook. Yet in the back of my mind, my self-worth and ability to lead my family came into question. This was a time for me to challenge myself in a different but less stressful way. I did not have anyone reporting to me and was instead simply reporting to myself.

During that time in my life, I also learned that it's okay not to be okay, but it's not okay to stay that way. For a time, if I am honest, I *did* struggle, as evidenced by this excerpt from my journal on December 21, 2016:

> **It's okay not to be okay, but it's not okay to stay that way.**

Well, nothing short of a "shitstorm" starting with getting taken out of the president job after four and a half years. I don't think any singular event has rocked my ego and confidence more. I have always placed a very high rating on humility as a character trait, but this situation has humbled me in a big way.

As I reflect, although it still stings, I think it will help me recover and rebound and is a great reminder that one should never get too cozy, cocky, or secure, no matter what job you have or what company you work for.

Despite the residual bitterness, I am thankful for the support of some salary coverage and healthcare for our family while I figure out what is next. That allows me to spend more time with the kids, take some special trips, get my health back on track, and learn how to network.

Along the way, I met some great and interesting people, many of whom I now call good friends. Despite the intermittent and gnawing inner chatter, I had said yes to my current circumstances and got pretty decent at it. Aside from networking, I did not exercise much strategy during my time out of the grind. To be honest, one of the many lessons learned from going through this personal exodus was the value of constantly networking. Prior to being forced to find another horse to ride, I had been a lousy networker. A lack of discretionary time made it difficult to focus on meeting people outside my former role. I also, probably naively, felt disingenuous taking time out of my day-to-day schedule to meet other people. Networking, however, is one of the most important things you can do, whether in building a career or taking a breather. I made it my job to get out and network—so much so that Jodi questioned what I was doing meeting with all these new people.

Networking creates opportunities. I was making some good connections and reacquainted myself with David, whom I met a couple of years before on the golf course while working at Worthington. David was the fifth generation of the Williams family and leader of Tri-W group, an organization created under his leadership to reinvest his family's proceeds from selling the majority of their business, W. W. Williams, founded in 1912. While getting back in touch with David, I shared the idea I had to purchase a company myself, and he graciously offered to support my endeavor. I ultimately did make an offer on a nice manufacturing business based in Columbus, Ohio, that fit my strength zone with the backing of Tri-W. Unfortunately, we finished second with our offer, but it opened up another door for me to help Tri-W and David continue to grow.

I initially joined David at Tri-W in December 2016 as a consultant to help them find businesses to purchase. One thing led to another, and I ended up joining the company full-time in mid-2017 as a partner to David and another colleague of ours, Nick. At age forty-eight, I saw another setback turned into a comeback. As a team, we set out to create a long-term strategy for Tri-W as a private family investment group that predominantly invests in value-added real estate and manufacturing and distribution companies. My position initially focused on building a marketing strategy and website and finding companies to buy.

Had I sat back and allowed fear to stop me from building my network, having business conversations, and taking another step on the path of my professional development, I would have allowed myself to stay stuck. There is a quote by George Brown, "Many times the best way, in fact the only way, to learn is through mistakes. A fear of making mistakes can bring individuals to a standstill, to a dead center. Fear is the wicked wand that transforms human beings into vegetables." Drawing out this line, "Fear is the wicked wand that transforms human beings into vegetables," my dad reminded my siblings and me that people who never make mistakes never accomplish anything. They seem bound by the fear of being perfect. We need to weigh our problems, know the pitfalls and risks, then weed our way through them.

Pause for Reflection: Soul Searching

For every season, there is a time. Soul searching is important, and as the nurse so lovingly and firmly reminded me, so is time with family. While sitting down to work on my book, patterns throughout my life started to become quite clear, especially as it relates to seasons. Have you ever written out the timeline of your life, with all its peaks and valleys, seasons of darkness, and seasons of joy? I bet you would find some valuable lessons and some periods of pure gratitude, love, pride, and joy.

I learned all too quickly how important it is to live in the moment, whether you're facing the loss of a job or a cancer diagnosis. I had to force myself to slow down and reflect. I had to take time to get all the junk out of my head, to put it on the side. Taking that step expanded my capacity to open up and fire off different neurons held hostage by stress in my brain. It has made me a more peaceful and thoughtful listener and decision-maker.

When you are going through your own setback, do not be in such a hurry to run to the next door. Instead, step off that hamster wheel for a breather. Every change, every setback, creates an opportunity for you to find that special role or special place you are designed for.

That is why I am here with you. I have wandered in the wilderness, and I am finding my strength zone, my gifts. I am listening to God, and he is guiding me on this new path to speak, to teach, and to guide.

Every change, every setback, creates an opportunity for you to find that special role or special place you are designed for.

It is not the money or the title. What drives me, what feels good to me, is inspiring people to grow, helping them develop their skills in business and life, turning setbacks into comebacks, and saying yes to opportunities.

CHAPTER 12

FROM SEIZURE TO OPEN CRANIOTOMY TO DIAGNOSIS

Can you give me superpowers while you're in there?
Or maybe some skills to play a piano or guitar?
—Andy Billman (to my doctor
during an open craniotomy)

Flash Forward: "Hey Andy, how're you doing?" I blink a few times as I hear my name and subtle noises I don't recognize, slowly opening my eyes to see a grayish-blue tent hanging in front of me. "Andy, you doing okay?" I attempt to move my body from this uncomfortable position, but I can't move. Then I remember. I'm in surgery. My brain is literally open right now as the doctors and nurses are talking to me. *Holy cow! This is so strange!* Nothing hurts. I can't move. My brain is open, and I can speak. "I'm good." One of the nurses asks me my kids' names. That's easy.

"Ellie, Ryan, Emily, and Owen." The questions continue, "What's your favorite color? Favorite food?"

When there is a break in the questioning, I realize this doctor is literally inside my brain right now, so I thought I'd ask him a question. "Hey, Doc, while you're in there, you think you can give me some superpowers or maybe some skills to play piano or guitar?" I can't see him, of course, but I can sense by his response that he is smiling. I love using humor to lighten the mood and settle my stress. So I figured if it works for me, maybe the doc would enjoy a little humor. And then that was it. Lights out.

I wake up in my hospital bed and wonder if it was all a dream. No. It's real, all right. Very real.

Seizure Number 2

As I detailed in the first chapter, I experienced my first seizure in August 2018. That was my wake-up call seizure. Then came my second seizure, again in Memphis, on September 4, 2018, which dropped me to the floor and landed me in the ER. This I referenced as the full-blown seizure.

I did something foolish. When the doctors diagnosed the tumor and scheduled the surgery for October, they suggested I go on seizure medication. I don't like to feel dopey and try not to take any medicines if I can help it. The suggestion implied that I had some choice in the matter, so I asked if it was my option. You, dear reader, may have caught on and are starting to ask the famous question, "What are ya doin', Billman?" I was still getting my bearings on what all this meant. A guy's gotta ask.

In response to my question, the doctors explained, "Before you had what we call a focal seizure, where you were awake but could not find your words. This would be a complete on-the-floor, legs shaking, and you would be unaware of what's going on. And they typically don't last very long, but you have to be careful you don't hit your head." The doctors said I could choose to forego the seizure medication but be aware that the next time I have a seizure, it likely would be more severe. Being typical lighten-the-room Andy, I kind of laughed it off and said, "So you're saying I have a chance of not having one?" I figured I'd take my chances, which, of course, was not wise on my part.

There is a teaching point here: If you have stepped in a pile of you know what once, don't do it again. On occasion, we have all accidentally tripped and stepped in two piles because that is just what was straight ahead on the path, out of our control. But this was different. I did this knowingly, probably deep down hoping that the path ahead was not what I feared and that this was all a bit of a fluke, despite initial scans showing otherwise. I'm not the brightest bulb around, but I can usually learn life's hard lessons.

This time around, however, I pushed my luck. The fact is, I had my second seizure, again while traveling on an early flight, again having more coffee than water, and again being slightly dehydrated. I was also flying with one of the same partners who had accompanied me during my first seizure a few weeks earlier.

As we started walking through the plant, I felt fine despite the 95-degree heat. My partner asked me what I thought, what I wanted to do this morning. My response was my modus operandi, something to the effect of, "Let's get out there and help the team get more organized. Let's lead by example."

There we were, out in this hot plant, picking up trash and lending a hand wherever we could. I was talking and laughing with my partner when my senses kicked into high gear. I suddenly felt dizzy, light-headed, and just not right. *I've seen this movie before! I am not going to have another seizure event today.* I got as far as inside the office, just enough time to sit down on a chair and take a swig of water. Our sales leader, Jeff, was talking to me about a customer opportunity off to the side. That was the last thing I heard before the seizure took hold.

This second seizure gave a new meaning to "man down." I guess it knocked me off the chair and onto the hard linoleum floor. As I have continued to hold my college lineman weight, I am sure the world heard it when I hit the ground! (I still tell people today that the reason I keep my body weight up is you never know when the NFL is going to call and need a good center.) All joking aside, this second seizure freaked out both my colleagues and me. Although seizures like this typically do not last very long, sometimes only a few minutes, they nonetheless can be violent, with lots of shaking around, shoes coming off, and more. Thankfully, I did not hit my head on anything on the way down to the floor.

When I awakened from this full-seizure event, my partner, Nick, was helping to hold me up while the EMS team worked to get me on a medical stretcher to transport me to the ambulance. I vaguely remember being strapped to a medical gurney as they rolled me out of the office. I don't remember much about the ride in the ambulance, other than being incredibly thirsty—like *Sahara Desert* thirsty. One of my partners rode along with me. We ended up at the same hospital, St. Francis Hospital in Memphis. Maybe it was punishment for complaining about the food the first time around. At the minimum, I should have received a "frequent guest card" for being back in the same hospital. They admitted me for observation, gave me fluids, and put me on anti-seizure medication immediately. Thankfully, this stay in the hospital was less dramatic as I knew what was happening and that it was something serious that needed expert care.

My partners had called Jodi when they first put me in the ambulance. I told her to stay home, that I would catch a flight back home after I got out of the hospital the next morning. While the staff admitted me, my partners, Nick and David, were vehemently arguing over who would get to babysit Andy and stay with him in the hospital. I don't recall a lot of the back and forth between them at the time, but somehow David prevailed. I think he said something like, "I'm shorter than you, so I'll fit on the roll-out chair better than you will!"

You probably already know what I did before getting out of the hospital the next day and back on a plane. I took a quick shower in the hospital and went with my partners to visit a separate supplier we had committed to see this time back down in Memphis. I know you're probably thinking, "What a *#$@! ass," and you would be right to think that. I knew I had to do something about the tumor in my head, but at the same time, my upbringing and football experience kicked in. *Yeah, your head might hurt, but your feet still work!* I planned to go to the meeting, get back home, move up the surgery, and get it taken care of. I am sure my partners thought I was nuts, but I can be quite convincing when I want to be. We made it through the meeting, and I flew home that night and prepared for the upcoming surgery.

Open Craniotomy

As a result of my second seizure, they moved up my surgery to September 25, 2018, at OSU. After the open craniotomy surgery and waking up in a recovery room, I saw my wife and my oldest daughter, Ellie, and her husband, A.J. At that time, A.J. was in his second year of residency at a hospital system in Akron, Ohio. They had my head all wrapped up from the surgery, and I vaguely recall talking with them and thanking them for coming down to be with us. I knew A.J. would need to get back to work at the hospital.

He and Ellie were not the only people who showed up that day. The entire immediate Billman family and spouses were present, along with Jodi's mom and dad. That is just the way our family rolls. And along with my family was our pastor from our church. After he prayed for a successful surgery, I thanked him for being with me before they took me back into the operating area. I will never forget the huge smile on his face as he looked back at me and said something like, "Andy, I've never seen so many people show up for a surgery. You are definitely loved by a lot of people."

Now, you might be wondering about the quote at the chapter beginning (my questions to the surgeon during the open craniotomy). Yes, I was awake for the procedure, and I just could not help myself. Here I am, strapped to a table with half of my brain wide open, and they had woken me up medically in the middle of the surgery so the doctor could get me talking. I just could not resist being a smart ass—always my go-to strategy for dealing with a stressful situation. I am not so sure the surgeon found my quips as humorous as I did, but I do recall him saying something back to me like, "Sorry, it doesn't work that way."

Final Diagnosis

My final diagnosis would be malignant anaplastic astrocytoma, WHO Grade III, IDH 1 wildtype, MGMT hypermethylated. According to the University of California San Francisco Brain Tumor Center, an anaplastic astrocytoma is a rare malignant brain tumor (accounting for about 1–2 percent of all primary brain tumors) that arises from astrocytes, the supportive cells in the nervous system. Also explained by the UCSF Brain Tumor Center, an anaplastic astrocytoma might also be called a glioma, or high-grade glioma.

Human functions that are impacted and symptoms that arise from this type of brain cancer are wide-ranging and dependent upon the location and size of the tumor. If the tumor is blocking the normal flow of the brain's cerebrospinal fluid, pressure can build, leading to headaches, nausea, and vomiting. Other examples of impairment include eyesight (if the tumor is near the vision center), weakness in an area of the body (if the tumor is near the motor cortex), and speech impairments (if the tumor is near the language regions).

Treatment for this type of brain cancer is very personalized and can include surgery, chemotherapy, and radiation. The type of each treatment option and the order of treatment are dependent upon a variety of factors. A multidisciplinary team of neurosurgeons, neuro-oncologists, and radiation oncologists considers tumor size, location, the extent of surgical removal, and how the patient is responding to treatment.

In my own words, the prognosis is not what a patient wants to hear. The statistics give me one year to five years. There is no cure. As you might have gathered, my outlook does not match my reality. Instead of looking ahead and fixating on what tomorrow looks like, I am taking one day at a time. Let me share my (quite repetitive) reality:

First, my treatment regimen has consisted of taking archaic chemotherapy drugs. On a Monday, I go in and get inside an MRI machine. Technicians will inject dye into me and will take all these pictures of my brain. Then I will get on an airplane and go to a business that I've invested in, and there I will work. When I return home, I will see my doctor, who will pull up images of my brain while my wife holds my hand. We learn very little new information about my cancer, only whether it is stable, growing, or not growing.

Instead of looking ahead and fixating on what tomorrow looks like, I am taking one day at a time.

Pause for Reflection: Wise Counsel

Pay attention to your body! As I reflect on all that happened leading up to the diagnosis of having a tumor in my brain, I could have helped myself by paying closer attention to what the doctors I met with were telling me rather than plowing forward, continuing to travel out of town, and resisting taking seizure medication.

When in your life have you not listened to wise counsel when it involved an important decision?

When something gets out of balance in your life, pay attention to how you feel and how you are reacting to how you're feeling.

The world might be pushing you to be more, do more, and try harder, but if you are feeling physically ill or overly stressed, take the time to gather some healthy and fresh perspective.

Take the time to slow things down and develop a plan to move forward from whatever is holding you back.

CHAPTER 13
WAKE UP. SAY YES. KEEP GOING.

My feet don't have cancer.
—Andy Billman

Flash Forward: Now, this is the life. Little Drew sitting on one leg. Little Will on the other. Moments ago, nothing my wife and I tried seemed to soothe their fussing. But this? This is like magic. I'm driving our golf cart just fast enough to feel a slight breeze on our faces. The sun is shining, hugging us in its warmth. There are so many sights and sounds coming at us from every direction that my grandchildren hardly know what to do with all of the stimulation except smile and laugh. We hear dogs barking, birds chirping. We see neighbors walking and squirrels scrambling up trees. We even see an alligator in the distance crawling out of the swamp. It's like we're on our own little safari adventure in this quaint, peaceful, friendly neighborhood on the coast of South Carolina. I can hardly hold the tears in as joy overflows my heart. I'm breathing. I'm living. I'm loving. I'm laughing. For a moment, I forget I have brain cancer. This is the life I want to live—every single day.

It is spring 2021. Millions of people in our country are finally getting vaccinated in an effort to end the coronavirus pandemic. My heart goes out to those who have lost friends and family members to COVID-19. What a year it has been for us all as we adjust to wearing masks everywhere and doing what we can to get back to normal. I continue to do my best to avoid getting sick from this virus while still fighting my underlying disease.

As of this writing, my condition is stable while the doctors keep eyes on my situation. That means I am in an MRI tube every six to eight weeks as my particular disease tends to "take off." No one knows why or when. I have overcome the "scanxiety" of getting frequent brain MRIs, and I have accepted the fact that, as of right now, there is no end in sight. I am encouraged and motivated to do everything I can to help myself and others who are fighting their own battles.

Throughout my life, whether it was my childhood, the game of football, my business career, or my battle with brain cancer, I have learned to adapt, and I have grown in every role and situation. I control what I can control, and I let go of what I cannot control. For example, I cannot control if treatment will work, but I can control when and how I show up. I cannot control how the tumor impacts my language, but I can control what tools I use to overcome the challenge. This is all especially true as I navigate my current storm. You cannot tell on the surface just how much I have weathered and how much I had to adjust, cope, and evolve.

A good example (as I *literally* put words on a page) is that I struggle with finding words, both in speech and in written form. This is a direct outcome of having brain surgery and post-surgery radiation. This challenge, in many ways, has been the toughest adjustment throughout this entire predicament. I used to be a voracious reader and was halfway decent using the written word to communicate to others. Now it is a daily struggle, especially in my line of work. I get frustrated quickly when I forget a word or how to write an email properly. But I have learned to find or create tools and strategies to overcome these obstacles. (My wife thinks I am dating this mysterious lady named Siri.)

As we near the conclusion of this book, I want to share some of the tools I hope you will take with you on your journey. I have not mentioned all of the ways that I am continuing to live. My friends and readers, *that* is one of the most important ideas I can impart to you—regardless of the obstacle, maintain forward momentum by taking action.

Even if it means letting the little old lady with the blue hair pass you, promise me you will keep putting one foot in front of the other. Did you promise? I need you to promise.

If I had decided to stop living, lie down on the couch, and accept the sleepless nights, the headaches, the pain, and the fear, I have no doubt the disease would have taken hold and progressed much more quickly. I also need to be real with you here. I have days where doubt creeps in, and I wonder if this is the year I will die and leave my wife and family behind. *Will this chemo drug beat this? What if I only have "x" number of days left on this earth?* Instead of staying in this state of mind, I work hard to flip my mindset into gratitude, turn pain into laughter, and turn fear into fight. I am fighting back, one day, one minute, one second at a time.

I am fighting back, one day, one minute, one second at a time.

One specific action I take is maintaining an "every-day-is-a-great-day" attitude. My father's good friend John Berg, who is now in his late seventies, served in the Vietnam War and lost many good friends there. I once heard him say, "After my experience in 'Nam when I thought I was going to die every day, I decided the day I made it back home I'd never have a bad day again." That statement had an emotional impact on me and cemented my understanding of how precious life is.

Along the way, I am sure you have put together that I am continuing to work, whether at the office, from home, or over Zoom. I'm also still jumping on planes to travel to business locations outside of the state. It makes me feel normal and allows me to continue adding value to my team, which is very important to me.

Would you have guessed that in 2019 (yes, post-brain-cancer-diagnosis), I went on a forty-five-mile bike ride with Emily to raise money for cancer research? You bet I did. Let me tell you, *ouch*! But it was worth it—every minute, every drop of sweat, and every ache and pain. It was another reminder of how important it is to have a goal out in front of me through every season in life.

As of late, in addition to loving our grandkids and keeping up with our children, Jodi and I have been working on our transition from Ohio to South Carolina. I have learned that I feel better mentally and physically when I can see the sun and feel its warmth. With each of these actions, I am taking action against my cancer. I am turning setbacks into comebacks. Forward momentum is, in essence, the definition of a comeback, right?

Enough about me, let's check in on you.

✓ What season are you in?

✓ What are you doing?

✓ Who are you with?

✓ What are you facing?

✓ How are you doing?

✓ And are you adjusting?

Many of you have dealt with or are dealing with some form of obstacle, storm, or life-changing event, whether an injury or health diagnosis, job loss or change, a relationship issue, or crisis. It can be especially difficult when there is a lack of closure. When it comes to my brain cancer, there is no cure. If I am brutally honest and completely vulnerable here—I don't want this to be a Pollyanna story—I am suffering from a lack of closure on my cancer diagnosis. I want a full diagnosis and prognosis. *I want to know.* And I cannot know. Sometimes, in the midst of a storm, we just don't know when it will pass or if a ship is coming.

We have to figure out what we need to survive the storm.

Say yes. Keep fighting. Keep trying. Stay positive. Stay active.

The storm will pass when it passes. There will be closure when there is closure. Do not close the book on yourself. (Yes, that's one pun I needed to keep, and I want it to stick.) Whether you're facing cancer, job loss, or the death of a loved one, giving up cannot be an option.

When a trial of seemingly insurmountable odds happens, many will lose their will to live, lose their sense of purpose and meaning, and give up. They begin worrying that they won't make it through it, or in more blunt terms, they will die. Here is the deal: All of us are going to die. But we do not know when, and I believe that's a good thing.

Back to you. There are options. There is hope. Help yourself as much as you can. There are some things within your control, and there are some things you have no control over. For example, answer the following questions:

✓ Are you moving your body? If so, how? If not, how can you start?

✓ Are you putting the right nutrition into your body? Sugar feeds most cancer. I am not saying eliminate sugar fully, but can you cut back?

✓ If you are not getting enough sleep, can you start your wind-down one hour earlier and perhaps shut down the technology earlier as well?

✓ And how about your mind? Do you have a nurturing routine for your mind too? Never forget the power of a positive attitude.

From the questions above, create action steps for yourself.

✓ Move, take a walk, maybe lift some weights.

✓ Eat healthier, say no to soda and candy bars, and say yes to more protein and fiber.

✓ Improve your sleep, set an alarm one hour before bed, and begin your wind-down exactly when that alarm buzzes.

Elevate your mindset, try reframing your situation. Do you lack the motivation to go out and walk?

Remember that some people with certain conditions can't take that walk.

✓ If your condition doesn't impact your feet, then use them, one foot in front of the other, adding an extra step each day.

✓ If you can't use your feet, do a push-up or roll your wheelchair forward. Read a book or even write a book! Find your strength zone within your mindset, and then metaphorically put one foot in front of the other in your own unique way.

I want you to know that I continue to struggle with all of these areas each day. I am in the middle of trying to be more active, eat healthier, and improve my sleep. My body weight is not where it should be, so this is a focus area for me. One morning I walked a mile and a half to a coffee shop because we were out at home. I could have jumped in my car, but instead, I turned it into an opportunity to get some fresh air and exercise. It comes down to taking baby steps in the right direction to help yourself. Believe me—I am here with you in that struggle. We are in this together.

When you turn the page, yeah, this guy has brain cancer. So much craziness in this story, whether the football challenges, the injuries, losing his investment in his company, or being fired from his job. The point is that everyone has challenges and craziness in their stories. Brain cancer became a blessing of sorts in my story. When I meet people or speak to an audience, I tell them, "I have brain cancer, it's a blessing, and here's why," and I share a story of hope.

I often ask audiences a series of is-this-you questions, such as, "Raise your hand if you've been touched by cancer." Do you know how many people raise their hands? Everyone. How many have blown out a tire, had an issue with a child, had an appliance break down, or some other issue that pops up in the board game of life? The point is, the perfect day is rare. Something will always be going on; an obstacle will always pop up. It does not have to take a major life obstacle like brain cancer to wake you up. For me, however, it led me down a path of enlightenment. It brought a new perspective on what it means to be alive and breathing and get to be around family for another day. It renewed my motivation, and if I am honest, it made me think deeply about how I want to spend my time and with whom. It gave me a greater purpose, and now my legacy includes not only my family but helping others—like you, dear readers—face their obstacles. You can be a part of my blessing!

Most importantly, I have learned that we all have a choice. We can walk our path and simply react to the setbacks we face, or we can choose to act in the face of those setbacks. We can think about having a bad day or focus on making it a good day, no matter what.

Let's own our stories, control what we can control, and make the most of every minute.

Pause For Reflection: Action and Time

What do I want you to do with this information?

FIRST: I want you to feel inspired. I want you to take charge and take action. I want you to figure out what you can control and make key changes.

If you have a bad habit that's not helping your situation, eliminate it.

This process takes mental energy and a positive attitude. The more you practice it, the more you master it. You can't give up. You have to keep trying.

Find your why. Pursue your passion. Master your energy to make it happen.

AND NOW: I'd like to bring my book back full circle. I've used a bit of a football metaphor as it relates to "seasons." If you could humor me one last time, I'd like to challenge you. None of us want to be benched or on the sidelines, but sometimes that's the next play in our game of life. Ready or not.

You have an opportunity, right now, to take an inventory of your time.

✓ How are you using it?

✓ How do you want to use it?

✓ Have you thought about how life can change when you least expect it?

Okay then, if you were given one to five years, would it change how you use your time? How? Sharpen your edge by having a game plan and building your body and mind every day, so you are ready for whatever competition or injury is ahead. Define what success means for you.

Now, get back in the game of life, help your team, and leave *nothing* on the field.

FAMILY REFLECTIONS

If there's one thing I've learned in life, it's to fight.
Fight for what's right. Fight for what you believe in,
what's important to you. But most importantly, fight
for the ones you love, and never forget to tell anyone
how much they mean to you while they're still alive.
—Author Unknown

Along the way, you have learned my children's names and
have gotten to know Jodi a bit. Here is where I can offer
you closure on what makes me tick, my reason for fighting.
Family.

Time is a strange thing. It ticks by at what seems
like a snail's pace when we are kids, even young adults.
Then, something switches, and it seems to fly by so fast
we sometimes miss out on being fully present in the
moments that matter, moments with our loved ones.
With major life events that remind you of your mortality,
such as preparing to head into surgery, it seems easier

to be fully present, easier to take note of little details. It is the mundane moments when we go through the motions and might forget how precious and tricky time can be if we are not intentional about making the most of every moment and relishing every detail.

I am so thankful for my family. Going through the process of writing this book has been a blessing on its own. Looking back and remembering all the fun times we have had together and hopefully, God willing, that we will continue to have going forward has been rewarding and priceless. I relish all our family traditions: the trips, the special way we celebrate everyone's birthdays, Christmas, New Year's, along with our many pool parties. My entire family has been with me throughout all the ups and downs of my life, especially over the last couple of years as I have had to adjust to my "new normal."

A final note to my wife and kids:

As you all know, this book came together with your gentle encouragement to say "yes" to writing a book. At first, I thought of simply writing each of you a hand-written note to express my deep love for you. I quickly realized, however, that the love I have for you all is inexpressible in mere words. Genuine love is a feeling that comes from down deep within you and never goes away. Regardless of the outcome of this nasty disease, thinking about my love for you gives me an unexplainable measure of comfort. It will always be there, whether I am or not.

Thank you all for nudging me along this journey to write this story. My desire is that it may be a reminder to us all that life can be fleeting, and we all need to cherish every moment of every day we have together.

Love you!
Dad

From Ellie (Billman) Yunker

In August 2018, I was a fresh, new mama to a beautiful baby boy. In the midst of those early days of parenthood, I learned of my dad's brain cancer diagnosis. I remember the fear and pervasive anxiety that weighed on my chest during those early days—beginning with that first seizure and leading to his awake craniotomy and eventual anaplastic astrocytoma diagnosis. For me, that fear was paralyzing at times. I remember rocking my newborn to sleep, sobbing, praying that he would have a chance to know my hero.

As you've read in the pages above, my dad has an otherworldly sense of vision and work ethic. Not surprisingly, he has approached his cancer and treatment with the similar strength of mind and body that he applied to football and his career. For my dad, turning setbacks into comebacks isn't just a clever mantra he used to title this book; it's a way of living for him. Because of my parents, my siblings and I have paramount examples in addressing the problems we all inevitably face in this broken world. They have grounded us in faith, modeled resilience in hardship, and cultivated the sense that hope is never lost. Hopefully, my dad's story brought some of those same things to you.

From Ryan Billman

What has it been like as your dad battles cancer?
The news has brought with it a wide and ever-expanding range of emotions. First, it was utter shock that this superhero-like symbol in my life was dealt a hand as horrible as brain cancer. The shock was quickly followed by a palpable fear that, to this day, I sometimes can't seem to shake. After receiving the bad

news that seemed to arise after every appointment and scan, the fear turned to frustration and anger. I just couldn't wrap my head around the question, *Why him? Why my dad? Why the man whose life has always revolved around pouring himself into others?* Out of all of these emotions, one rang truer than the rest: hope. One of my dad's most enduring qualities is that of perseverance. He has an insatiable desire to win and has always, with no exception, refused to lose. This trial of his was not going to be that exception. Whenever that fear creeps back in, I lean on that hope, knowing my dad will fight tooth and nail to win because that's who he is.

How are you doing/coping? What keeps you positive?

Looking back at this last year compared to when this all started, in a strange way, I feel blessed. I had been accustomed to bad news every time he would visit the doctor, and I dreaded those weeks leading up to a scan. I am thankful to have been gifted my father's optimism. But to be honest, this adversity chipped away that optimism piece by piece. It felt as if it were slowly overcome by pessimism. But as time progressed, stable scans started to gain a winning record over the bad news I was too familiar with. I wouldn't choose this way to learn a life lesson, but it was a life lesson nonetheless. No matter how dark things can get, there is always a little nugget of good, and that little nugget weighs a whole lot more than everything else. All we can do now is celebrate it, hold it close, and never let it go. As for positivity, I have my dad to thank for every ounce of it. I mean, how crazy is it that the man whose life was upended by brain cancer is the one fueling those around him with positivity? It is such a testament to his stand-out character. Aren't we supposed to be the ones helping him remain positive? Not to Andy Billman.

He strapped this unimaginably heavy burden to his back, put his head down, and kept on paving a path forward. To most, this diagnosis would stop them flat in their tracks, and rightfully so. But to my father, it is just a little speed bump, like he had a prolonged flu or something. It seems that every time we need a little positivity, my dad siphons it out of his own tank and tops us off. He has always put the needs of others over his own because that's who he is.

How would you define your dad?

How do you define a guy like my dad? Trust me; it's not as easy as it sounds because there is so much there. To sum up one of his many defining characteristics, I would say my dad embodies how God intended for us to love those around us. He makes whomever he is talking to feel like the most important person in the room because for that moment, whether short or long, you are the most important person in the room to Andy Billman. To take this a step further, he has always seen the best in everyone he crosses paths with. It doesn't matter who you are or what you've done; my dad almost unconsciously tosses the bad and zeros in on the good. Andy Billman doesn't just see the best in people. He brings out the best in people and has this unique ability to pour into others and make them better. To put it simply, he is the shining example of how I want to carry myself in life, how I want my future kids to carry themselves in life, and how God intended for us to carry ourselves in life. In our ever-changing world, most people have self-focused motives. Unfortunately, this modus operandi (MO) is so well ingrained in our nature. But Andy Billman doesn't subscribe to that way of life. It's not in his nature. His humble, caring, uplifting, and gentle soul doesn't have a motive. At his core, he just wants to help people be the best version of themselves because that's who he is.

What's a special or funny (or both) story you want to remember or want people to know?
Something that has always remained true throughout the many stories we have shared—my dad is a funny guy. Like a really funny guy. Like Will Ferrell type of funny guy. (Will is one of our absolute favorite actors.) I remember growing up always thinking that my dad was the most humorous of them all. Today, he still takes the cake. Even when confronted with a horrible diagnosis like brain cancer, he never lost that humor. Sitting next to him in the hospital room after his open craniotomy where a brain surgeon poked around his brain, the guy still made me laugh. During brain surgery, you have to be awake to make sure the surgeon doesn't cross a few wires and accidentally make you speak mandarin or something. My dad's surgeon is a VERY serious guy. I am sure it is a job requirement when you operate on brains every day. I remember my dad saying his only mission the whole surgery was to get him to laugh, and you bet he did. On a day as scary and stressful as that, my dad, medicated, exhausted, and may I add missing parts of his brain, still managed to make me laugh like he has since I was a boy. I just remember being overcome with emotions privately because my dad was still there. He wasn't missing any of the pieces that make him— well—*him.* You hear stories of people who undergo brain surgery and come out different. I can't lie; I had a very real fear of that. But Andy Billman came out the other side Andy Billman. When he made me laugh, that fear subsided, and it was quickly overtaken with the purest sense of peace because that's who he is.

What do you want your dad to know?

Dad, your humble nature will probably deny any of this, but you are my superhero and a superhero to countless others. I have never, and I mean NEVER, heard anyone say a bad word about you. You have an utterly profound impact on everyone you come into contact with. It's just infectious. How lucky am I to have a father like that? I mean it when I say, "God's greatest gift in my life is you." I don't deserve it, but I am not giving it back! He gave me a winning ticket when he put me under the care of two of the most amazing parents, teachers, cheerleaders, advisors, and coaches I could ask for. You have patiently walked, run, picked me up when I've fallen, and sent me into life. Yet you have never left my side. You just give, give, and give some more as if it wasn't enough. Sometimes I just want to scream, "*I don't need any more. You have given enough!*" But I know you; you would just give a little bit more and then some. Dad, you didn't just cross off all the typical "dad" checklist items . . . teaching me to ride a bike, hold the door open for girls, work hard, never give up, blah blah blah. Just like everything you do in life, you went above and beyond the "call of duty" as a father. You taught us what a healthy marriage should look like and how to love and support a spouse unconditionally. You taught us the profound importance of reputation and how easily it can be compromised. You often paired this lesson with the words, "When you carry yourself day-to-day, you're not just representing Ryan, you are representing the Billman name." You taught us the value of tenacity and perseverance, telling us always to work harder than the person next to us. You taught us the importance of having family and faith at the heart of everything we do. With this and too many other lessons to count, you taught us how to pass on all of these things to another generation. So, in essence, Dad, you impacted so many generations to come, so many Billmans to come. If that's not the most special thing, I don't know what is. Talk about a legacy. I could go on and on with examples of how you have given us the world, or at least the skills to capture it. But at the end of the day, I just hope you feel like the most accomplished guy in the world because, in my eyes, that's what you are. And that's who I want to be—Andy Billman.

From Emily Billman

If you've ever met Andrew Billman, you'll undoubtedly agree with every word I am about to write. And if you haven't, I'd like to paint a picture for you.

For my twenty-third birthday, all of my best friends surprised me in my hometown, which obviously meant a trip to the Billman's. At one point, I was talking with my best friend at the kitchen counter when I looked over to see every single person in the room, other than us, sitting on the floor around my father, intently listening with wide eyes as he was telling life stories and the lessons he had learned from them. One of them in particular had tears in her eyes while he was speaking. In high school, if any of my friends were going "through a valley," as we like to call it, the Billman house was a safe place, and Andrew Billman was always there to listen, process, and provide discernment.

He emulates the perfect picture of a father figure to so many. People are naturally drawn to his wisdom, humbleness, and gentle spirit.

I've been very open about my struggles with my father's diagnosis. It's been a process of learning how to cope with our family's "new normal" for the last three years. There have been many tears, night terrors, and waves of grief, but it's also been a season where I experienced the most growth. The hardest part has been preparing myself to potentially lose a father—and not just a father, but the only person I've ever met that is as close as it gets to perfection. Of course, no one is perfect, but man, does Andrew Billman walk close to that line. When I look at the Bible and the characteristics of God as a Father, I can't help but think that my dad embodies all of those things. He is a refuge. He is gracious. He is merciful. He is forgiving. He is a helper. He is a shepherd. He is compassionate. He is loving. And he is giving.

All of this is to say that I am so thankful the Lord gave me an earthly father who loves me unconditionally but is also a picture of the Heavenly Father to many others.

I will fight with you and for you today and every day. I love you a bushel and a peck and a hug around the neck, Dad.

From Owen Billman

It sounds cliché, but I truly believe there can be superheroes in one's life. I am thankful that I have one—my dad. I have been alive for twenty-one years, and I still have yet to come across a person who has half of his qualities. Over the last few years, I have grown closer than I ever have been with him. When I think about him, the first thing that comes to mind is his humble attitude. He has been such a successful man and has accomplished things that some may never in a lifetime. Another quality I see from him is his willingness to see others succeed. I've seen this time and time again through how he treats us kids, as well as through the stories I've overheard about his workdays. Finally, one of the most important qualities a person can have is the willingness to put their head down and work their ass off through the easy obstacles and the most difficult ones. Dad has this quality, and he has shown it, and it has flourished ever since he stepped foot on this earth. I love how he can have these amazing qualities and still be the best dad out there. One summer, my family spent a week in Positano, Italy. I had a monumental moment with him—our first beer together. This memory is something I will hold on to for the rest of my life. Dad, I love you and will love you till my grave. You are not just my father; you're my rock and our family's rock. You are my hero and my inspiration that keeps me moving through the mountain of life.

Pause for Reflection: Family

Who do you consider family? When you think of making the most of every moment, who are you spending time with? Who do you fight for? Most importantly, who do you need to remind how much they mean to you, and what do you need to say?

> Life is precious. Don't take a single second for granted.

Make a list of the most important people in your life, write down a few thoughts about each one, and then simply connect.

Life is precious. Don't take a single second for granted.

Practice Failure

We learn valuable lessons when we experience failure and setbacks. Most of us wait for those failures to happen to us, however, instead of seeking them out. But deliberately making mistakes can give us the knowledge we need to more easily overcome obstacles in the future.

—Farnam Street Media

APPENDICES

PLAYBOOK TO WIN AT THE GAME OF LIFE

Andy's F6: My Quirky and Simple Approach to Approach Life

Faith—Believe in something bigger than yourself.

Faith in God first and faith in yourself second can often provide the proper perspective to handle anything coming your way.

Family—Remember what is really important in life.

We all get distracted at times, too focused on work and making more money. After your faith in who created you, family is what matters. Families are complicated, just like we are all complicated as individuals. It takes real effort to stay together and support each other, but it's so worth it in the long-term.

Fitness—Take care of your health, energy, and confidence.

Regardless of your body type, we all need to move more. Staying active is a natural way to improve your outlook, no matter what you are currently facing. It gives you the energy and capacity to attack life in a positive way.

Finance—Secure your future and independence.

This is not about being fixated on money. It's about being a good steward of what you've been given. When you save money for a rainy day, preparing ahead for what might come your way—whether a blown tire or the loss of your job—you will have peace of mind.

Friendships—Nurture meaningful and authentic relationships.

The focus here is authentic relationships. Like you, I'm blessed to have some great relationships, including some lifelong friendships. It's important to understand the difference between an authentic relationship and a casual acquaintance.

Fun—Enjoy life.

If you're not having fun, what's the point? Don't take yourself or others too seriously. Life is hard enough, so find a way to enjoy the life you've been given.

Andy's Words of Wisdom

I shared with you in the book how I have enjoyed reading and learning along the way. I have collected many motivational quotes and insightful thoughts in my many journals through the years. Some are original, some come from the people whose words have touched my life, and some I simply can't remember where I picked them up. But as I reflected on them, I was reminded of the power of words, and I wanted to share some of my favorite words of wisdom with you.

I have often reflected on these words, especially during times of uncertainty in my life. My wish is that something here will inspire you or help you work through a situation in some way.

- ✓ Do four important things a day, and start by making your bed—leaving only three main things to accomplish for the day.

- ✓ Nobody is going to row your boat. You have to do the work!

- ✓ "The most important conversation you could have is with yourself, and the most important person you have to lead is yourself." —David Goggins

- ✓ Get comfortable being uncomfortable because that is how you will grow.

- ✓ Listen 90 percent of the time and speak 10 percent of the time.

- ✓ Don't underestimate the importance of a good night's sleep.

- ✓ Daily formulas for success:

1. Show gratitude.

2. Pray.

3. Spend forty-five to sixty minutes of your day getting some physical activity.

✓ Be done with being great. Do all the little things to be elite, whether at school, working at a company, or in your family.

✓ Retirement is a farce.

✓ Positivity wins!

✓ You are either a maker (giver) or a taker.

✓ Have the attitude that if you wake up tomorrow, you'll never have a bad day.

✓ People are beautifully messy.

✓ Pay attention to what people do, not what they say.

✓ Everything in moderation—except *love and hugs* for your family.

✓ Build a reserve in your bucket that sustains you during tough times.

✓ Shine a light on what is right!

✓ Separate how you feel physically from what you need to get done.

✓ "A man is about as big as the things that make him angry." —Winston Churchill

✓ The difference between successful people and exceptionally successful people is the latter says no to just about everything.

✓ If you can't explain something simply, you don't really understand it.

✓ We may not know the future, but we know who does; therefore, we have every reason to wait with courage, certainty, and confidence. God promises to give courage and strength to those who wait upon him.

✓ "Some cause happiness wherever they go; others whenever they go." —Oscar Wilde

✓ All it takes is all you've got.

✓ Grit. It's all about GRIT!

✓ Ten things that take 0 percent talent but will get you 100 percent respect:

1. Punctuality

2. Work Ethic

3. Effort

4. Body Language

5. Energy

6. Attitude

7. Passion

8. Coachability

9. Generosity

10. Preparation

✓ Cancer is a great teacher.

✓ Live a life worthy of your calling.

✓ The more coachable you are, the faster you will get better.

✓ Be humble enough to receive feedback, even if it hurts. You can get better, or you can protect your ego, but you can't do both.

✓ Don't be defensive or combative. Understand that all feedback and coaching come from imperfect people.

✓ Actively seek feedback about your strengths and weaknesses, as well as ideas for improvement.

✓ Be where your feet are. Be present and connect deeply with people.

✓ Don't be selfish; don't try to impress others. Be humble, thinking of others as better than yourselves. Don't look out only for your own interests but take an interest in others too. —Philippians 2:3–4 (NLT)

✓ Ask, "What is God calling me to do?"

✓ Don't worry when you face opposition. Worry when you don't.

✓ We are not defined by our circumstances, jobs, possessions, or positions in society. Instead, we are defined by who we are in Christ.

✓ Learn to listen. Listen to learn.

✓ "I don't want to be a great problem-solver. I want to avoid problems—prevent them from happening and doing right from the beginning." —Peter Bevelin

✓ "He suffers more than necessary, who suffers before it is necessary."—Seneca

✓ "The greater danger for most of us lies not in setting our aim too high and falling short; but in setting our aim too low and achieving our mark." — Michelangelo Buonarroti

✓ Mistakes are as serious as the results they cause, understand this, my dear brothers and sisters; you must all be quick to listen, slow to speak, and slow to get angry (James 1:19).

✓ "There are seven days in the week, and 'someday' is not one of them."—Benny Lewis

✓ "The power of a man's virtue should be measured not by his special efforts, but by his ordinary doing."
—Blaise Pascal

✓ "You will waste your cancer if you treat sin as casually as before." —John Piper

✓ "Are your besetting sins as attractive as they were before you had cancer? If so, you are wasting your cancer. Cancer is designed to destroy the appetite for sin."—John Piper.

✓ "Pride, greed, lust, hatred, unforgiveness, impatience, laziness, procrastination—all of these are the adversaries that cancer is meant to attack. Don't just think of battling against cancer. Also, think of battling with cancer. All these things are worse enemies than cancer." —John Piper

✓ Six Ethics of Life:

1. Before you pray—Believe

2. Before you speak—Listen

3. Before you spend—Earn

4. Before you write—Think

5. Before you quit—Try

6. Before you die—Live

Neal's "Words of Wisdom"

These notes from my dad have kept me going since the early 1980s when he shared them with us. He would write a quote from another source and then write the meaning in his own words. I still have these hand-written notes today. I hope you, too, will find encouragement in them.

> The following are just a few of the many thoughts I gathered over the years. They all have some special meaning and were used at one time or another to help inspire players to do better.
>
> I thought it might be good to share the meaning of them with you. Others might intepret them differently, but so be it. I really think they are good lessons to learn or live by, or at least refer to from time to time.
>
> If you think about it, most of these ideas or thoughts have been taught by your mother on a day-to-day basis.
>
> Love, Dad
> Dec. 25, 1980

• • •

"Man cannot discover new oceans unless he has the courage to lose sight of the shore." —Andre Gide

Never be afraid of the future or what it might hold. Plan, explore, and reach out beyond yourself. Don't ever shackle yourself with negative thoughts—at least not for very long.

• • •

"The road to success runs uphill, so don't expect to break any speed records." —Jim Tressel

Success at anything takes time, patience. Chip away daily, weekly, and keep chipping!
If it was easy (whatever this thing is you want to do) it wouldn't be worth doing. Don't be afraid to do hard things; they're more fun in the end.

• • •

"The successful man lengthens his stride when he discovers the signposts have deceived him. The weakling sits down and complains." —Unknown

When your best plans fail, go faster, get at the problem. Just don't whimper and feel sorry for your mistake. Obstacles are just more challenges to your character. You will not be without obstacles. How you face them is the real issue!

• • •

"No man can defeat us unless we first defeat ourselves." —Dwight D. Eisenhower

Winning or losing happens first in the mind—before any external threat. By our thoughts we become our first and toughest foe.

• • •

"Are you captain of an uncharted dream?" —Unknown

Are you in control of your goals? If you set goals, you only need to follow your plan and soon they will be achieved.

• • •

"On the beach of hesitation bleach the bones of countless millions who sat down to wait, and waiting, died." — George W. Cecil

Go do the thing now! Be decisive. More people die mentally, long before they die physically. Bite off more than you can chew, then chew it.

• • •

"Never give in. Never give in. Never, never, never, never—in nothing great or small, large or petty—never give in except to convictions of honor and good sense." —Winston Churchill

Why sacrifice your principles—all you know to be right? If you give up on the small ones it just makes it easier to give in on the great ones. The majority of people will compromise a lot for little. These are not tomorrow's leaders or the winners of today.

• • •

"In the long run, men hit only what they aim at." —Henry David Thoreau

Select your target (goal), take aim, and concentrate. Hitting the target (goal) is never an accident. It's always planned and well thought out or imagined!

• • •

"A Winner"

- Never blames others for his failures.
- Is positive.
- Isn't boastful.
- Sets realistic goals.
- Isn't surprised to win.
- Is a dreamer . . . and becomes one.
- Works.
- Does all the things a loser won't do.

—Unknown

• • •

"Many times the best way, in fact the only way, to learn is through mistakes. A fear of making mistakes can bring individuals to a standstill, to dead center. Fear is the wicked wand that transforms human beings into vegetables." —Unknown

People who never make mistakes never accomplish anything. They seem bound by fear of being perfect. Weigh the problems, know the pitfalls and risks, and weed through them.

• • •

"Some men see things as they are and say, 'Why?' I dream things that never were and ask, 'Why not?'" —George Bernard Shaw

Most people are afraid of change. But where would we be today if somebody didn't say, "Nuts, I'll do it!"? Everything starts from a dream.

• • •

"Good habits are not made on birthdays, nor Christian character at the new year. The workshop of character is everyday life. The uneventful and commonplace hour is where the battle is lost or won." —Maltbie Babcock

People who know you, see you in action day to day. You build character over a lifetime . . . you have to work at it.

MEDICAL RECORDS DETAILING ANDY'S CANCER JOURNEY

Whether you are a fellow cancer survivor, a medical professional, or someone simply interested in what brain cancer looks like through a medical lens, you are welcome to read through the technical journey (my medical records), broken into four bite-size parts on the following pages.

MEDICAL NOTES: 08-09-18 through 12-26-18

Initial Presentation: Mr. Billman is a fifty-one-year-old Caucasian male who was evaluated by Dr. E. in the neurosurgical oncology clinic on 08-09-2018 for a brain lesion. He reported he had been traveling out of state for business and experienced lightheadedness, visual disturbances, including colors in his field of vision, which he attributed to fatigue. He was also noted to have some difficulty responding to his colleagues. He had difficulty remembering their names and was also disoriented. He was taken to urgent care in Tennessee, where he was at the time and subsequently transported to a local hospital. He was evaluated for a possible stroke and had a cardiac and stroke workup performed. The patient was seen for a follow-up visit on 10-08-2018.

It was noted at the time of that visit that on 09-04-2018, he was in Tennessee and was seen in a local ER after a seizure.

• • •

On 09-25-2018, the patient was status post awake left temporal craniotomy for resection of brain tumor, performed by Dr. E. The pathology was consistent with anaplastic astrocytoma, WHO Grade III. He reported some occasional dizziness and numbness in his right thigh. He had a dull headache. He reported some persistent confusion, decreased concentration, and sleep disturbance. He was about to stop his steroid medication. He had some difficulty finding words and spelling. I personally reviewed the images associated with the brain MRI performed on 08-21-2018 (associated with a Functional Brain MRI):

"Infiltrative, non-enhancing intra-axial tumor involving cortex and juxtacortical white matter of the left posterior inferior temporal lobe. Tumor shows low corrected rCBV—. Appearance is compatible with a low-grade glioma, most likely astrocytoma. Tumor shows indistinct margins, including a somewhat vasogenic edema-like signal at its medial aspect, which extends in close proximity to underlying white matter tracts. There is probably some tumor infiltration at the lateral aspect of the posterior left ILF, as well as at the inferolateral aspect of the proximal left optic radiation. Left hemispheric lateralization on 4/4 language-related tasks. Activation in the posterior portion of the left superior temporal gyrus and in the posterior portion of the left superior temporal sulcus extends immediately adjacent to the superolateral aspect of the tumor. Additionally, activation on the covert naming task, along the inferior aspect of the left inferior temporal gyrus and left fusiform gyrus, extends adjacent to the inferomedial margin of the tumor."

• • •

I recommended radiation and temozolomide chemotherapy followed by six cycles of temozolomide. I reviewed the pathology, including the molecular and genetic profiling of the tumor, the treatment schedule (Stupp regimen) with possible associated risks and side effects, and the possible alternative of clinical trial participation. The patient was also seen in Radiation Oncology on the same date to start treatment planning for his disease. He was also counseled about treatment by Mary S., RPh, Pharm D in clinic. He was advised not to drive, climb heights, operate heavy machinery, or swim until otherwise advised. He expressed understanding and agreement to comply. He was also urged to be compliant with his anticonvulsant and to avoid sleep deprivation and alcohol consumption.

• • •

The patient was seen for a follow-up visit on 12-31-2018. He was status post completion of chemoradiation on 12-03-2018. He received 60 Gy in 30 fractions to the left temporal tumor bed. He tolerated the treatment quite well. He was evaluated weekly in radiation oncology and neuro-oncology nurse practitioner clinics during the treatment. He reported mild daily headaches, responsive to simple analgesia. He denied dizziness, tremors, seizures, difficulty with his speech, focal weakness, or focal numbness. A brain MRI was performed on 12-26-2018.

MEDICAL NOTES: 01-17-19 through 03-28-19

The following report was noted: "Evolution of post-surgical changes involving the lateral left temporal occipital parenchyma as detailed above. Hyperintense FLAIR abnormality involving the adjacent parenchyma likely representing neoplastic disease with superimposed post-treatment changes appear similar to the prior study. Contrast enhancement along the margin of the surgical defect has decreased. No other interval changes are demonstrated."

We discussed the next steps of his care, which would be to proceed with adjuvant cycles of temozolomide in 5/28 day schedules. We discussed that the dose administered was higher than the one given to him and doing radiation therapy. We also discussed that this may result in some increased side effects during the days of administration, especially nausea and emesis. The patient was made aware that he will need to see us on a monthly basis to prescribe the chemotherapy and will need to get a brain MRI every eight weeks to assess the tumor bed.

• • •

The patient was seen in the neuro-oncology nurse practitioner clinic after completing cycle 1 of adjuvant temozolomide. He reported that overall he was doing well. He did report an increase in fatigue but denied any nausea or constipation. He denied any seizure activity. He asked about going to the dentist and having a colonoscopy in terms of timing. He was planned to start cycle 2 of adjuvant temozolomide on 02-04-19.

A brain MRI was performed on 02-25-2019. I reviewed the study, and the following report was noted: "No significant interval change compared with the prior study. Redemonstration of post-surgical changes involving the lateral left temporal occipital parenchyma as detailed above. Hyperintense FLAIR abnormality involving the adjacent parenchyma likely representing neoplastic disease with superimposed post-treatment change appears similar to the prior study. Minimal contrast enhancement along the margin of the surgical defect also appears similar." He was advised to start cycle 3 of temozolomide, return to clinic in one month, and have a brain MRI performed in eight weeks.

• • •

The patient was seen in the nurse practitioner clinic on 03-28-2019. It was noted that he had started cycle 3 adjuvant temozolomide on 03-03-2019. He had tolerated the cycle without significant side effects, other than some increased fatigue, but had continued to work full time. He denied any seizures since September 2018. He denied any new or worsening neurological symptoms, such as focal weakness, visual changes, or changes in sensation. He was advised to proceed with cycle 4 of adjuvant temozolomide 200 mg/m2 with a tentative start date of 03-31-2019. He was also advised to continue on levetiracetam ER 2000 mg at bedtime, which was well tolerated without significant side effects or breakthrough seizures.

MEDICAL NOTES: 04-25-19 through 09-09-19

The patient returned for a follow-up visit on 04-25-2019. There were no new major concerns. There was some fatigue associated with the chemotherapy cycle. He did have occasional dizziness. He reported having a brief spell associated with missing one of the doses of levetiracetam. This consisted of significant distortion of his vision and some disorientation the day after missing a dose of the anticonvulsant in the evening. He did not have any additional episodes after that. He denied having any focal weakness or numbness.

A brain MRI was performed on 04-22-2019. The study was reviewed, and the following impression was noted: "No significant change from prior MRI from 2-25-2019." The patient was advised to start cycle 5 of temozolomide and return to clinic in approximately one month to start cycle 6. A brain MRI was planned following cycle 6 of chemotherapy or in approximately two months. He was aware that with any seizure episodes, he must not drive for at least six months following the episode. He was also very well aware of sensible seizure precautions to protect himself and others were he to lose control or consciousness. He was in agreement to comply.

● ● ●

The patient returned to clinic for a follow-up visit on 07-02-2019. He described occasional dizziness and occasional mild headaches, which were happening about every other day. He had noted that he had occasional word-finding difficulty but no difficulty with comprehension. He denied any seizures. He also denied tremors, weakness, lightheadedness, or numbness. A brain MRI was performed on 06-24-2019 and was associated with the following report: "New small contrast-enhancing foci within the left temporal occipital parenchyma which are nonspecific. It is unclear whether these foci are due to neoplastic process or post-treatment change. Attention on follow-up is recommended. No other interval changes are demonstrated. Redemonstration of post-surgical changes involving the lateral left temporal occipital parenchyma. Hyperintense FLAIR abnormality involving the adjacent parenchyma likely representing neoplastic disease with superimposed posttreatment change appears similar to the prior study. Minimal contrast enhancement along the margin of the surgical defect is unchanged."

It was discussed with the patient and his family that the differential diagnosis included tumor progression versus treatment-related changes. The areas were too small for perfusion assessment. We discussed that although a biopsy was possible, it might also be prudent to get close follow-up imaging in approximately one month. The patient was agreeable with this approach. He was advised to return to clinic on 08-01-19, with a brain MRI scheduled for 07-29-19. He was also advised of seizure precautions until the exact nature of the underlying brain abnormalities had been determined. Levetiracetam was increased 750 mg twice a day from 500 mg twice a day, and he was advised to seek immediate medical attention for any new symptoms. He was in agreement. I also advised that I would discuss the patient's imaging with the other team members, including neurosurgery and radiation oncology, preferably in a tumor board setting.

• • •

The patient returned to clinic for a follow-up visit on 08-05-2019. He continued to do well clinically and did not have any new symptoms. He continued to have very occasional and very mild word-finding difficulty. He denied any definite seizure activity. He was occasionally forgetful. He had not developed any focal weakness or numbness and continued to take his anticonvulsant medication. As had already been discussed with the patient and his family since his previous visit with us, the patient's case was discussed at tumor board on 07-08-2019. There was consensus that a close follow-up brain MRI was appropriate, especially since review of his radiation treatment plan with his radiation oncologist during tumor board showed the new areas of enhancement to be within the treatment field.

A brain MRI was performed on 09-03-2019. I reviewed the study and noted the following report: "There is evidence of progression of the abnormal enhancement as noted above with an increase in FLAIR signal changes as well. Previously noted enhancing lesions have increased in size, and there are new foci of enhancement within the temporal lobe and hippocampal region." We discussed with the patient and his family that he did not appear to be symptomatic from those areas of enhancement. There were factors that pointed towards possible tumor progression in these areas (moderately elevated perfusion) and others that favored treatment effect/radiation necrosis (The patient is not specifically symptomatic from these areas; they are within the radiation field. The tumor had a methylated MGMT gene promoter and especially for the larger lesion, an appearance possibly consistent with necrosis.) We did discuss that the options at this point would be close follow-up with a brain MRI in approximately one month, proceeding with a biopsy to establish the diagnosis, enrollment in a clinical trial based on the assumption that these areas represent tumor progression or treatment of a clinical trial based on the same assumption.

The patient's preference was to do close follow-up imaging and advise us immediately if he were to develop new symptoms. I thought this was a reasonable approach, especially since in discussing his case with Dr. E., it did appear that there were significant risks associated with a needle biopsy of the larger lesion in question. The two clinical trials discussed included OSU 16264, Phase I Trial of Hypofractionated Stereotactic Irradiation (HFSRT) combined with Nivolumab, Ipilimumab and Bevacizumab in Patients with Recurrent High-Grade Gliomas and Study to Evaluate Eflornithine + Lomustine vs. Lomustine in Recurrent Anaplastic Astrocytoma (AA) Patients (not available at our institution but available at OhioHealth). The former study poses risk of possible continued radiation damage if the imaging changes noted are consistent with radiation-related changes. The patient and his family clearly understood the complexity of his situation and were agreeable with the management plan.

• • •

The patient returned to clinic on 09-09-2019 for a follow-up visit, accompanied by his wife. Since his previous visit with us in early August 2019, he had obtained opinions from other institutions. He had been seen at the Cleveland Clinic and OhioHealth. He had not been started on any treatment for possible progression. He also had telephone contact with Duke University Medical Center, where his images had been reviewed. In clinic, the patient reported one episode of sudden dizziness that was felt to be a possible seizure by the neuro-oncologist at OhioHealth, and the patient's anticonvulsant dose was increased. Otherwise, he had occasional word-finding difficulty, which was stable and chronic.

A brain MRI was performed on 09-03-2019. I reviewed the study and noted the following report: "Interval increase in size of contrast-enhancing abnormalities in the medial left temporal parenchyma around the margin of the trigone of the left lateral ventricle. Surrounding FLAIR abnormality is also mildly increased. A few other foci more laterally are also new/more prominent than on the prior study as detailed above. It is unclear what part of these interval changes are due to progressing neoplastic disease versus post-treatment change. New focus of non-enhancing hyperintense FLAIR abnormality in the left frontoparietal periventricular, white matter with indeterminate etiology. Small focus of enhancement within the superior left cerebellar hemisphere region and which may be within a sulcus. This focus appears slightly larger than on the prior study and new compared to the study previous to this. Although nonspecific, this focus may be due to post-treatment change given the location below the tentorium cerebelli. Attention to this area on continued interval follow-up MRI is recommended. Redemonstration of post-surgical changes involving the lateral left temporal occipital parenchyma."

I had a counseling session with the patient and his wife regarding the imaging findings and the best plan moving forward. The imaging was discussed first. I advised the patient and his wife that the continued increase in the previously noted areas of enhancement and the appearance of new areas is certainly concerning for possible progressive disease. However, it is noted that for at least one of these areas, treatment-related changes were specifically reported to be more likely. Given the fact that the patient was possibly symptomatic (possible seizure), I did suggest proceeding with available therapeutic options, including the clinical trial available through OhioHealth. I discussed his imaging with neurosurgery and confirmed that a biopsy of the periventricular lesion carried risk of potential intraventricular hemorrhage and other potential risks.

The patient was agreeable to contacting the neuro-oncologist at OhioHealth regarding proceeding with the clinical trial. I contacted the neuro-oncologist at OhioHealth personally to make sure that he was aware that the patient would be seeking a close follow-up appointment to possibly proceed with consent signing and study treatment. Otherwise, the patient was advised to continue on the new anticonvulsant dose as prescribed by the outside neuro-oncologist, continue to follow seizure precautions including no driving, and present to the emergency department with any new symptoms, especially seizures or severe headaches.

MEDICAL NOTES: 12-19-19 through 08-07-20

The patient returned to clinic on 12-19-2019 for a follow-up visit. Since his previous visit with us in September 2019, he was evaluated at OhioHealth, started on a clinical trial titled "Study to Evaluate Eflornithine + Lomustine vs. Lomustine in Recurrent Anaplastic Astrocytoma (AA)," enrolling on the control arm and was subsequently continued on lomustine off trial when a brain MRI showed possible progression. The MRI was performed on 10-10-2019. This was during the first cycle of the lomustine on trial. He was continued on lomustine off trial. He is about to complete cycle 2 at this time and reported that he should be starting cycle 3 on 12-25-2019. In clinic on 12-19-2019, the patient reported fatigue. However, his main symptom was severe hand and leg cramping that seemed to be mostly nocturnal. He had positional dizziness occasionally and daily dull headaches.

A brain MRI was performed on 12-16-2019. I reviewed this study and noted the following report:

"Redemonstration of contrast-enhancing abnormalities in the medial left temporal parenchyma around the margin of the trigone of the left lateral ventricle. Surrounding FLAIR abnormality also appears similar. Stable small focus of enhancement within the superior left cerebellar hemisphere. Redemonstration of postsurgical changes involving the lateral left temporal occipital parenchyma. Paranasal sinus disease/changes. New air-fluid level in the right maxillary sinus suggests acute sinusitis. Clinical correlation is recommended."

The patient was advised to continue lomustine and was to start cycle 3 on 12-26-2019. He was to return to clinic on 02-06-2020. A brain MRI was scheduled for 02-03-2020. He was to discontinue use of CBD oil and related products that he had been using for insomnia to see if the cramping would go away. We planned on an insomnia prescription if he did not see improvement and asked our pharmacist to check for possible interactions between tricyclics and his current medications. Magnesium and iron levels were checked to assess possible other causes for muscle cramping. We discussed a peripheral neurology referral to assess for neuropathy/myopathy if cramping persisted. We also advised the patient to monitor for clinical signs of sinusitis.

• • •

The patient returned to clinic for a follow-up visit on 02-06-2020. He was quite symptomatic. He described fatigue, and his wife reported that she had noticed that he was quite short of breath for the past two weeks. He had also developed a dry cough. He denied having any hemoptysis. The neurologic review of systems was positive for an episode of confusion that happened about three weeks prior to the visit. The patient apparently could not remember the name of a very familiar person. He also continued to have some occasional word-finding difficulty as well as cramping in his hands and legs. He had a headache, which was fairly constant at this point.

A brain MRI was performed on 02-03-2020. I reviewed this study and noted the following report: "Stable size of contrast-enhancing abnormalities in the medial left temporal parenchyma around the margin of the trigone of the left lateral ventricle. Surrounding FLAIR abnormality also appears stable. Stable separate tiny contrast-enhancing foci along the lateral margin of the trigone of the left lateral ventricle and in the posterior lateral left temporal lobe. Stable small foci of enhancement within the superior left cerebellar hemisphere. Redemonstration of postsurgical changes involving the lateral left temporal occipital parenchyma."

A venous doppler of the lower extremities and a CT scan of the chest with pulmonary embolism protocol were requested for high suspicion of deep venous thrombosis and pulmonary embolism. We also requested pulmonary function tests to assess for possible pulmonary toxicity from lomustine. The patient was advised to continue on same anticonvulsants since it was unclear if the episode of confusion represented a seizure. This was also an isolated event.

• • •

The patient was called on 04-16-2020 for a telephone visit. Since his previous visit with us, it was noted immediately after the visit that the venous dopplers and CT scan of the chest with pulmonary embolism protocol indicated deep venous thrombosis in the lower extremities and a large, saddle pulmonary embolus. The patient was immediately referred from the CT scan suite to the emergency room to start anticoagulation emergently and observation for a 24-hour period once these results become available. An echocardiogram was unremarkable. He was discharged on rivaroxaban. The patient also indicated after this admission that he needed a break from chemotherapy. This was felt to be reasonable so that he was off treatment at the time of the visit on 04-16-2020.

• • •

I reviewed a brain MRI performed at the Medical University of Charleston on 04-06-2020. I also noted the following report: "Likely residual glial neoplasm centered in the left occipital lobe peritrigonal white matter measures up to 3.5 cm. There are also two small nodular enhancing subcentimeter foci in the left temporal lobe, which are suspicious for tumor. Please note, no prior MRI examinations or history is available. Should prior examinations become available, we can addendum this report. Few punctate foci of enhancement in the left superior cerebellum, which are indeterminate. Recommend correlation with prior imaging and attention on follow-up."

A brain MRI was requested in approximately two months, and the patient was to continue staying off tumor-directed therapy. He was to continue on the same anticonvulsant treatment. The patient had also agreed to continue anticoagulation.

• • •

The patient was called on 05-28-2020 for a follow-up visit. He reported doing quite well, especially if he had had a good night's sleep. On days when he had not slept well, he noticed some word-finding difficulty. He also continued to have discomfort when lying down. He describes pain in his abdomen and chest that resolves very quickly when he stands up and paces around. His wife had noticed that he also had some occasional discomfort reported when he was standing. This was mainly chest discomfort but was much milder and rare, according to the patient. The patient also described that his short-term memory had been slightly worse since he has tapered off the steroids.

A brain MRI was performed on 05-26-2020. I reviewed the study and noted the following report: "Redemonstration of contrast-enhancing abnormalities in the medial left temporal occipital parenchyma around the margin of the trigone of the left lateral ventricle. Allowing for differences in technique between exams, the surrounding T2-weighted signal abnormality also appear stable. Additional separate tiny contrast-enhancing foci more inferiorly and laterally in the left upper lobe and the left cerebellar hemisphere, most of which are also unchanged. There are a few tiny new nonspecific areas of contrast enhancement in the lateral aspect of the left temporal lobe. No other interval changes are demonstrated. Redemonstration of post-surgical changes involving the lateral left temporal occipital parenchyma."

The patient wanted to maintain the same clinical and imaging surveillance and have another brain MRI and visit in approximately eight weeks. He was started on methylphenidate 5 mg in the morning for two weeks and then increased to 10 mg in the morning. The patient was called on 08-11-2020 for a brief telephone visit. He reported that he was being helped by the methylphenidate started at the time of his most recent previous appointment. However, he felt that he might need a slightly higher dose. He continued to have headaches on and off. He denied seizure activity, changes in strength or sensation on either side of his body, or changes in his ability to think clearly.

• • •

A brain MRI was performed on 08-07-2020. I reviewed this study and noted the following report: "Some of the areas of enhancement along the posterior and inferior resection margin are slightly more rounded and nodular in morphology. This may be related to evolving treatment-related changes. Surrounding T2 signal abnormality has mildly improved. No imaging evidence to suggest local tumor progression. Continued imaging follow-up recommended."

The very slight changes noted on the brain MRI were discussed with the patient via telephone; we discussed that it would be prudent to obtain the next MRI in one month instead of two, and the patient was in agreement. The dose of the stimulant was increased to

10 mg daily to be taken in the morning. The patient preferred to hold off adding additional treatments for headache prophylaxis since he felt that these headaches are mild, and he did not want to risk the side effects of the medications used to treat them.

BIBLIOGRAPHY

Chapter 1

Muccino, Gabriele, dir. *The Pursuit of Happyness*. 2006; Sony Pictures, DVD.

Chapter 2

Eliot, George. "Count That Day Lost," 1887.
McRaven, Admiral William H. "This One Simple Secret Will Change Your Life Today." YouTube. August 17, 2017. Goalcast Video, 6:00. youtube.com/watch?v=3sK3wJAxGfs.

Chapter 7

Alfange, Dean. "My Creed." United States Congressional Record, 1952.

"Entrepreneur's Creed." International Entrepreneurs Association (IEA), 1976. Adapted from "My Creed" by Dean Alfange.

Chapter 11

Brown, Bruce Eamon. 1001 Motivational Messages and Quotes for Athletes and Coaches: Teaching Character through Sport. Monterey, CA: Coaches Choice, 2000.

ACKNOWLEDGMENTS

The inspiration for this book came from my wife, Jodi, and our four kids, Ellie, Ryan, Emily, and Owen, as I faced the biggest setback of my life—being diagnosed with an obscure malignant type of brain cancer in late 2018. After recovering from brain surgery and learning the news from the pathology, I became reflective about what matters in life. Facing the reality of life's fragility brought the kind of focus and understanding to my life that I had never felt before. As I contemplated my future living with brain cancer and my own mortality, I could not help but think about all the things I wanted to tell my family and friends. My family encouraged me to write a book rather than simply writing everything down in my personal journal.

This book is a result of that gentle nudge from my family. Having never written a book, I was nervous at first and insecure about sharing my story with the world.

Here we are, almost two and a half years later, and we have our first book!

I am so thankful for all the encouragement along the way to say *YES!* to sharing my story here. My sincere hope is that this book will, in some way, however small, help someone else facing their own setback.

A special thanks to my loving family and faithful, longtime friends, former teammates, and colleagues for standing by me throughout this journey while fighting this disease and working on this book. I could not have done this without the faithful and consistent support of the people I love the most. I would also like to thank the team at Igniting Souls Publishing Agency and especially Teresa Alesch for her amazing support and patience in delivering this manuscript.

Say *YES!*

Andy

ABOUT THE AUTHOR

Andy Billman believes in the power of saying, "Yes!" Over his lifetime, he's faced various obstacles that he reframed into opportunities he could learn and grow from. His most recent "yes" was to a stage-three malignant brain cancer diagnosis in 2018. Faced with this mountainous challenge, Andy's past, present, and future crystallized into a sense of clarity most people do not achieve in a lifetime.

Andy is the author of *Setbacks into Comebacks: Saying Yes! to Overcoming Challenges and Embracing Opportunities.* His mission is to help people find hope and take action by saying yes to winning at the game of life, especially in times when it feels easier to give in, withdraw, and sleep away the pain, fear, and overwhelm. Instead of saying, "It's over," Andy says, "It's the beginning. It's what you make of each moment." Through his writing, speaking, and coaching, Andy helps individuals identify what is most important to them, find the courage to say yes, and then choose to live fully with the people who matter most.

Former president of Worthington Cylinders, a $1.1 billion global manufacturing leader, Andrew J. Billman now focuses on investments at Tri-W Group, a private family investment group. Andy earned his bachelor's degree in business from Miami University, where he played football and was a team captain and a three-year letterman.

Andy defines himself as a husband, father, football player, speaker, leadership coach and trainer, and author with a passion for helping others realize they don't have to experience cancer to find clarity and true happiness in life. He loves spending time with his wife, Jodi, and their four children, Ellie, Ryan, Emily, and Owen, along with their spouses and growing bundle of grandchildren.

BLAZE NEW TRAILS TO SUCCESS WITH ANDY BILLMAN'S LEADERSHIP TRAINING

Your business' strength is its leadership and team.

Grow yours into an unstoppable powerhouse.

Whether you need one-on-one or team training, Andy Billman personalizes your training to escalate your road to success by showing you how to:

» Harness the power of perspective.

» Transform challenges into new opportunities for growth.

» Lead from the front.

» Empower your team to reach new levels of success.

Schedule a consultation today
AndyBillman.com

YOU DON'T HAVE TO LEAD ALONE.

Andy Billman shares his proven strategies to empower your team and accelerate growth by:

» Developing skills to help you push through setbacks and transform them into opportunities.

» Cultivating a culture of growth-mindset and positive thinking in the workplace.

» Discovering tools to help you live your best life, personally and professionally.

Hire Andy as your Leadership Team Coach today.
AndyBillman.com

EMPOWER YOUR AUDIENCE
TO CONQUER OBSTACLES

Business leaders and their teams can face incredible challenges. Andy Billman reveals the keys to viewing them as opportunities to grow personally and professionally.

Andy is passionate about sharing his many years of leadership, business, and life experiences with organizations large and small.

Schedule Andy for your next event
AndyBillman.com

IS YOUR TEAM LOOKING FOR A CATALYST TO HELP YOU GROW?

Take It To The *Next Level* Today

Andy Billman equips leaders and teams to achieve remarkable results through his business coaching programs.

Contact Andy today to learn more!
AndyBillman.com

ANDY'S PLAYBOOK TO WIN AT THE GAME OF LIFE!

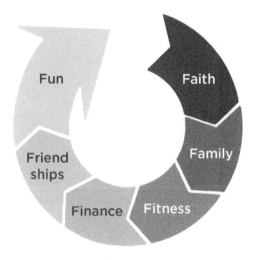

FAITH—Believe in something bigger than yourself.

FAMILY—Remember what is really important in life.

FITNESS—Take care of your health, energy, and confidence.

FINANCE—Secure your future independence.

FRIENDSHIPS—Nurture meaningful and authentic relationships.

FUN—Enjoy life!

DOWNLOAD YOUR FREE PLAYBOOK AT ANDYBILLMAN.COM TODAY!

Made in the USA
Monee, IL
14 December 2021